Advance Praise for *Jam Bake*

"When I make jam, a spoonful will go on toast, but after that, I always rack my brain trying to think of ways to use it in baking. Thankfully Camilla has done all the hard work for me. *Jam Bake* inspires with original combinations of jam—coffee with dates and pears, figs with plums and purple grapes—and brilliant baked goods to make with them. It's an indispensable resource for anyone who loves making jam and baking in equal measure."

BEN MIMS, cooking columnist for *The Los Angeles Times*

"Everyone needs jam in their lives, and cake for that matter—Camilla Wynne's passion for both has come together here in a book that is as much fun as it is informative and instructive. I mean who wouldn't want to make and eat apricot and cocoa nib jam followed by jam swirled brownies? This is the stuff that dreams are made of."

ANJA DUNK, co-author of *Do Preserve* and author of
Strudel, Noodles & Dumplings

"Camilla Wynne, the indefatigable chef, writer, and teacher, has blown my mind with this funny, sensual, and lively book. The recipes are clear and forthright; the treats are scrumptious and heavenly. As I am writing this, the nutty, irresistible scent of brown butter is flooding my senses— because as soon as I finished reading *Jam Bake*, I stood up, turned my oven on, and started making her pistachio blondies."

NATASHA PICKOWICZ, pastry chef and activist

"Thank goodness for this new triumph of a book, which provides not only recipes (and clearly-explained science and technique) for wildly creative jams, jellies, and more, but pairs them with a beautiful spectrum of cakes, pastries, cookies, and even ice cream! While jam-on-toast will forever be a classic for good reason, Camilla has given us all a much wider world in which to capture and celebrate the most beautiful bounty of each season."

ALLISON KAVE, author of *First Prize Pies* and *Butter & Scotch*

JAM BAKE

Inspired Recipes for Creating and Baking with Preserves

Camilla Wynne

appetite

by RANDOM HOUSE

Appetite by Random House® and colophon are registered trademarks of Penguin Random House LLC.

Library and Archives Canada Cataloguing in Publication is available upon request.
ISBN: 978-0-525-61108-0
eBook ISBN: 978-0-525-61109-7

Photography by Mickaël A. Bandassak
Food Styling by Michelle Marek and Camilla Wynne
Illustrations by Maggie Boyd
Book and cover design by Leah Springate
Printed and bound in China

Published in Canada by Appetite by Random House®,
a division of Penguin Random House Canada Limited.

www.penguinrandomhouse.ca

10   9   8   7   6   5   4   3   2   1

*This is dedicated to my parents for teaching me so much about
hard work and creativity, and for always supporting my choices 1,000%,
no matter what wild life path I choose to follow.*

"And the Quangle Wangle said
To himself on the Crumpetty Tree,—
'Jam; and jelly; and bread;
'Are the best of food for me!'"

—EDWARD LEAR

Table of Contents

Preserving 101   ## Baking 101

Standalones

Duets

Containing Multitudes

Base Recipes

Introduction

I'm somehow embarrassed to admit that I have a passion (not sure if that's due to my British heritage or being a teenage punk), but I'm going to be brave here and confess that I have three in fact. The first is cooking, under which fall preserving and baking. The second is teaching—something that I never thought I'd do but has become one of my favorite occupations. The third is reading and writing—the former I could do ceaselessly and the latter I have a more complicated relationship with, but both feed off one another and are nearly as important to me as food. Oh and wait, maybe a fourth: I could not live without fruit. It brings me boundless joy and inspires awe season to season. Fruit is primarily what this book is about—you won't find a recipe without it.

When I told someone I was writing this book, they said, "How niche." But to me, it makes perfect sense. I've been asked countless times, "What can I do with jam besides put it on toast?" It's a good question! But when you think about it, jam is literally at the heart of so many pastry classics—Linzertorte, rugelach, Pop-Tarts . . . the list goes on. What a pleasure, after all, in the depths of winter, to taste white peaches or sweet summer cherries. This is the delight that preserving affords us, and it goes hand in hand with baking. My career is proof of that.

I moved to Montreal thinking I would become a scholar, but eventually had to admit that nothing consumed my attention in the same way that baking did. Daydreaming in Latin and Russian Lit about cakes I might make, filling up notebooks with ideas. I eventually decided to apply to pastry school.

Fast-forward to when I was required to intern at a pastry shop or restaurant. In spite of being warned against it (I was told "vegetable-forward restaurants are just a fad," which seems hilarious now), I went to work at a beautiful restaurant called Les Chèvres with Patrice Demers, a pastry chef who was just a year or two older than me but already extremely accomplished (and who would only become more so). I would go on to work there on and off in their sun-filled pastry kitchen. It's where I first made marmalade.

I had also, though, joined a band. So when I left on tour, I left restaurants. We made three records and traveled around the world. To the annoyance of my bandmates, I would bring huge pieces of luggage to squirrel away culinary delights, get us lost or detained as we tried to go to recommended restaurants, and disappear after soundcheck to Paris pastry shops where I'd spend days' worth of hoarded per diems. I wouldn't trade that experience for anything. Slovenia's farmers' markets, Tokyo's izakayas, Texas's kolache bakeries—all these delights, plus getting to read all day and regularly being the recipient of applause, were heavenly. I didn't abandon cooking, though. During my times at home between tours, I honed my preserving skills, obsessively jarring my favorite, fleeting fruits and vegetables so that I could enjoy them at my leisure.

Then we played a show in Tokyo in 2009 and were never in the same room again. Breaking up had been a long time coming, but for a year I convinced myself we were just on a break. I started to work for my friend Stephanie Labelle, who was opening her incredible pastry shop, Pâtisserie Rhubarbe, and for my friend Michelle Marek, pastry chef at the time of a classic Montreal bistro called Laloux.

In 2011, I launched Preservation Society, which sounded much bigger than it was, since in the beginning it was me alone. I made jams, jellies, marmalades, chutneys, pickles, and fruits in syrup in unique flavor combinations using as much local produce as possible. I had no idea how to run a business, but I learned as I went, producing preserves with a cult following, hiring employees, and running workshops. Then the person I love decided to pursue a career that required us to move, and I learned how little fun it is to move a business. But fortunately I also remembered how much I missed pastry, and so I returned to my original calling. While I stopped selling preserves, though, I didn't stop making them or teaching others how.

I never set out to become a preserving teacher, but once I began I had total satisfaction sharing something I love with inquisitive students. As a self-taught preserver I had read every book on the subject I could get my hands on, but I found much of the information to be contradictory and that few of the reasons for why we followed the procedures we did were explained. This led me to Liberty, NY, for a Master Preservers course. I had a great time, but we were literally made to chant, "Canning is not creative cooking." As I was writing my first preserving cookbook at the time, this saddened me. I know the USDA guidelines for home-canning are made to reduce to the absolute minimum the risk of foodborne illness and contamination, but it seemed to me that folks could be given a little credit and allowed to make safe substitutions and additions to recipes.

To dive deeper into the science, I took two-week long classes on artisanal preserving at the Institute of Agriculture and Technology in Quebec, where I learned from experts more than I'll ever need to know—but most importantly I learned the streamlined method I still use for jarring jams, jellies, and marmalades (page 17). Now when I teach classes, my philosophy is that if you know why you follow the prescribed procedures, you won't make any terrible mistakes. So we start by talking about microbiology, just as we do in this book (page 7).

Once you really understand what you're doing, you can start getting creative. To me, creativity is one of the main delights of being alive, so I hope I've set you up here to make jam and bake with jam in a way that expresses something about you or your favorite fruits (page 33). Or you can just follow the preserving and baking recipes. I did, after all, write them for you. —CW

How to Use This Book

This book is designed to be indispensable to preservers and bakers alike. If you're a preserver, you probably have a cupboard bursting with jars of jam. I certainly do. Every year, without fail, I get overexcited at the farmers' market and end up biking home with my unplanned fruit purchases bouncing around in the basket and hanging from my handlebars (not a recommended way to transport delicate fruit, honestly). A batch of jam works out to about five jars, and so inevitably the golden raspberries, blushing gooseberries, and white peaches I couldn't resist all multiply into more jams than I can give away. So, if you're on the hunt for more ways to use your preserves, you've come to the right place. Each of the preserve recipes in this book is followed by two baking recipes that incorporate it.

And if you're a baker who's never tried their hand at preserving, I'm here to tell you it's easier and less time-consuming than you might think. It is highly likely you're about to become one of us, but if not, you can still bake all the baking recipes herein using a good-quality store-bought jam (page 34). Substitutes are suggested for each recipe in the notes section.

After we dispense with the science of preserving (page 7)—which delves into microbiology lite (page 7), the mystery of pectin (page 10), and the streamlined canning process (page 17)—and the art of baking (page 39) (which you need to know—don't skip it), we come to the recipe section. The preserve recipes are divided into three categories:

 Standalones (pages 52–74): Single-note flavors starring a specific fruit

 Duets (pages 78–150): Pairings that shine together

 Containing Multitudes (pages 154–224): Wild potions full of all sorts of fruits and more

Sometimes you just want to be able to whip something together instantly, while other times you want to sink your teeth into a big project. To help you decide, I've included difficulty levels for the baking recipes. They are indicated by the whisk symbol:

 Easy

 Intermediate

 Advanced

Don't be intimidated by the more difficult recipes, though. The more you challenge yourself, the better you'll get.

Preserving 101

The Art & Science of Preserving

In order to avoid ruin, it is paramount to learn the hows and whys of what is happening when you seal up fruit in a jar. That's the science. The magic comes once you have understood the science and can begin to explore your creativity safely.

Fear and Loathing in a Jar: Bacteria, Mold, Yeast, and Enzymes

After we've dispensed with introductions, the first thing I ask my students when I'm teaching a workshop is, "If you haven't tried preserving yet, why not?"

Some reply that it seems too complicated (it's not—see my streamlined method on page 17!). Some say you need all sorts of equipment they don't have (you don't—check out page 13!). Some say it takes too much time (no way—as illustrated on page 18!). But what I'm really waiting for is for someone to confess that they're afraid of killing their friends and family.

You are? Good! You should be, to some extent. There's a potentially deadly toxin that can, under the right conditions, be found in canned food. It's called botulism, and you're wise to want to protect your loved ones from it (or really anyone at all).

Now the scary thing about botulism is that there's no way of knowing if it's present in a jar. It doesn't look a certain way, it doesn't have a smell, it doesn't taste like anything, and it won't sing you a siren song. I like to say the only sense you can use to tell if botulism is present is your sixth sense! So unless you're psychic, it's a bummer.

Not only is this poison undetectable to the average person, it can also be fatal, in particular if you're very young, very old, or immune-compromised. But even a perfectly healthy person can succumb if they don't seek treatment soon enough. And either way you're getting very ill.

So at this point, I'm sure I've frightened you, but I don't want you to be scared, just informed. We must press on!

Botulism starts out as an innocent bacteria by the name of *Clostridium botulinum*, which lives in the soil. So if I go out to the backyard and eat one of the loganberries from my garden that has fallen on the ground (it's a new plant and we get very few, so I would definitely do this), it's possible that I'm putting some of this bacteria in my mouth. Do I die? Not unless I choke! It's only when this bacteria finds its ideal environment that it starts to produce the toxin that makes people sick.

Here are its three necessities:

1. A Vacuum *Clostridium botulinum* is an anaerobic bacteria, which means it needs an absence of air, a vacuum . . . like a sealed jar. Since we want to make shelf-stable jams, which must be sealed, that's not great.

2. Moisture Bacteria are just like us, they need water to live. So unless you're making a jar full of rocks or adding a *lot* of sugar (see page 9), we're still checking all the boxes.

3. A Low-Acid Environment This is the most important factor in preserving. Botulism can only grow in an environment where the pH is above 4.6. Do you have a pH meter at home? No? Well, you don't need one. The good news here is that *almost all fruit* is well below that pH, which means it's high in acid, which means we need have no fear of botulism whatsoever! The only way you could push most fruits into the danger zone is by adding a lot of really basic ingredients. Not basic as in pumpkin spice lattes, but basic as in the opposite of acidic. So don't make any jams full of Dutch process cocoa powder (nibs are better anyway—see page 32), baking soda, or Comet, and you'll be good.

Of course, we can preserve low-acid foods like meat, fish, soup, and vegetables, but this needs to be done in a pressure canner, which can achieve the very high temperatures at which botulism is destroyed.

Are you still scared of botulism? No! At least, not in the context of jams and marmalades. On the other hand, if someone gifts you a jar of home-canned soup, you might be a little wary, but you now know enough to ask a few specific questions about how they made it to determine its safety ("Did you pressure-can this?" "Did you follow a recipe from a trusted source?").

However, even if we know our preserves are high in acid, there are still some other bacteria, along with their friends yeasts, molds, and enzymes, that won't kill you but can still ruin your day if you don't follow the proper rules for sterilization (see page 20). Bacteria can cause slime, yeast can cause weird carbonation and outright explosions, and mold can cause, well, mold. Following the correct procedures will either kill or halt any of these potential offenders, leaving you with happy, healthy, shelf-stable jams.

By trusted source I mean a book published after 1994 that seems to have a good foundation in science. While there are good websites on canning, the Internet unsurprisingly contains a lot of misinformation, so be wary there. As for heirloom recipes, unfortunately they aren't always safe either. It's not that I don't trust your grandparents or your great-aunt Edna, but they were working with different ingredients than we have now—tomatoes, for instance, used to be safe to can straight up, but they have since been bred to be sweeter and less acidic, which means they now require additional acidification.

Sugar and Water: A Love Story

A lot of folks seem to think that adding sugar is essential to the safety of a jam. Not so! Safety-wise, sugar is entirely irrelevant, as long as you sterilize properly. Sugar does, however, play a role in the longevity of your preserves. The more sugar in a preserve, the better the long-term preservation of the color, taste, and texture. Too much sugar, however, and you can scarcely taste the fruit. It's a balancing act.

A student in her 60s at one of my workshops shared that she had been making jam for years without ever sterilizing her jars, with great success. Lately, however, every time she gave a jar of jam to someone, it turned out the surface was covered in a thick layer of mold. Not a great gift! (Fun fact: You can cut mold off hard things like a firm cheese and consider it eliminated, but if you scoop it off a liquid or a semi-solid like jam, invisible mold still remains, dispersed jellyfish-like throughout. It won't necessarily hurt you, but it's good to know it's there when you're deciding whether to eat it—informed consent!).

This made me think back to my grandmother's jam-making methods. She never, as far as I knew, sterilized her jars, but often reused old jars from store-bought jam. Yet her jams were always perfect, never moldy. Similarly, people used to "seal" their preserves with paraffin wax, a melted food-safe wax poured onto the surface of the jam. (If you don't remember it, I'm sorry, because pushing the disk of wax off the surface of a jam was one of the best tactile sensations I knew as a child.) However, jars covered in paraffin only look sealed to the naked eye. On a microscopic level, they are full of tiny holes plenty big enough for bacteria and mold to enter at will. So why wasn't there an epidemic of moldy jams?

It all comes down to what we call water activity. All fruits—and therefore all jams—contain water, which bacteria and mold both need to live (they really are just like us!), but sugar binds to water molecules and prevents

the bad elements from using them, creating an inhospitable environment.

It helps if you think about a preserve as a big high school dance. Sugar is attractive but jealous, the queen bee or the football captain. When sugar walks into the dance, it grabs a water molecule and essentially tells it, "We're going steady." If a mold or bacteria comes along and tries to cut in, the sugar just gives it a withering look that sends it packing. So if every water molecule has a sugar molecule for a dance partner, there's no chance of mold developing—it slinks out to go smoke cigarettes in the parking lot instead. This was the case for old-fashioned jam recipes that used equal or higher proportions of sugar to fruit. It didn't matter if you didn't sterilize your jars or if you sealed them with that imposter, paraffin. But if you want to make jams that are lower in sugar, there will be plenty of free water molecules in the mix, and they basically act like wallflowers waiting for someone to ask them to dance. And the thing about water is that it's very open to new experiences. It will dance with sugar, salt, honey, mold, bacteria . . . you name it.

For this reason, jars must always be properly sterilized, eliminating any mold and bacteria present and sealing out any that might come knocking in the future.

Speaking of honey, it's a delicious and potentially healthier alternative to sugar in jam recipes, and it can be nice to substitute some or all of the sugar for honey. But honey doesn't act like sugar at the dance. Think of it more as a laidback artist kid. Honey will dance with water, but if mold tries to cut in, honey just flashes the peace sign, says, "Cool, catch you on the flipside," and goes to hang out at the punch table with its friends from drama class. This isn't a problem for keeping the sterilized jam in your cupboard (although the shelf life won't be quite as long—honey doesn't safeguard taste, texture, and color in the same way as sugar), but once the jam is open in the refrigerator it will succumb to mold much more quickly than even a low-sugar jam. For this reason I always put up 100% honey-sweetened jams in half-size jars so we can get through them before they go bad.

How Does Pectin Work, Anyway?

Pectin is what makes jam gel. It's a naturally occurring polysaccharide in fruit, but different fruits have more or less naturally occurring pectin. So while you never need to worry about a Seville orange marmalade or quince jelly getting a proper set (unless you undercook or overcook them), because they are high-pectin fruits, some low-pectin fruits, like cherries and pears, don't gel so easily. In North America, there is a prevalent idea that all jam should be the same texture—so set that you can stand a knife up in it. I prefer to take the European approach, which allows for a range of textures, depending on the natural pectin level of the fruit. Don't worry—it won't slide off your toast! A low-pectin jam might just be a little looser.

High-pectin fruits include apples, citrus, currants, cranberries, crabapples, gooseberries, plums, and quince. On the lower end of the pectin spectrum are blueberries, cherries, peaches, pears, and strawberries. You must also take the fruit's degree of ripeness into account, however. The riper the fruit, the less natural pectin it contains. When I see old, sad, overripe flats of strawberries at the market labeled "jam strawberries" it fills me with dismay! If you're adding commercial pectin to them, that's fine, but since strawberries are already a low-pectin fruit, it will be near impossible to get a good set for them on their own when they are too ripe. Ideally, what we want is a mixture of 75% perfectly ripe fruit and 25% slightly underripe fruit.

Usually jam will set pretty well with almost any fruit as long as you're doing a normal at-home batch of four to five 250 mL (8 oz) jars. The moisture evaporates easily and concentrates the solids, so even if the spread isn't gelled per se, it's still thick. But some very low-pectin fruits can still need a boost if you want the jam to have a traditional firm set. For a long time I combined low- and high-pectin fruits to provide added gelling power, or I added a chopped (high-pectin) green apple to jams made from low-pectin fruits, which would all but disappear, yet help to contribute to a good set. Eventually I came around, however, to sometimes using commercial pectin to help me out.

Commercial pectin is fruit-derived, but I have long held prejudices toward how it's used. The masses of subpar jam on the market use added pectin to get a reliable set and to achieve a greater yield, causing the jam to set before much water has had the chance to evaporate. To my palate, the result often closely resembles Jell-O. Of course, taste is subjective, and folks who grew up on sweet, pectinated jam might like that best. I, however, like my jams rich and thick with concentrated fruit flavor and much less added sugar (around 50%) than required if you're using the standard commercial pectin, which requires a certain quantity for the chemical reaction to occur (80% or higher).

My trick, when I do use commercial pectin, is to use low-sugar or no-sugar pectin, neither of which require a large amount of added sugar, and to only add it once the fruits are properly cooked down and concentrated so the jam has the rich taste and texture that I always seek.

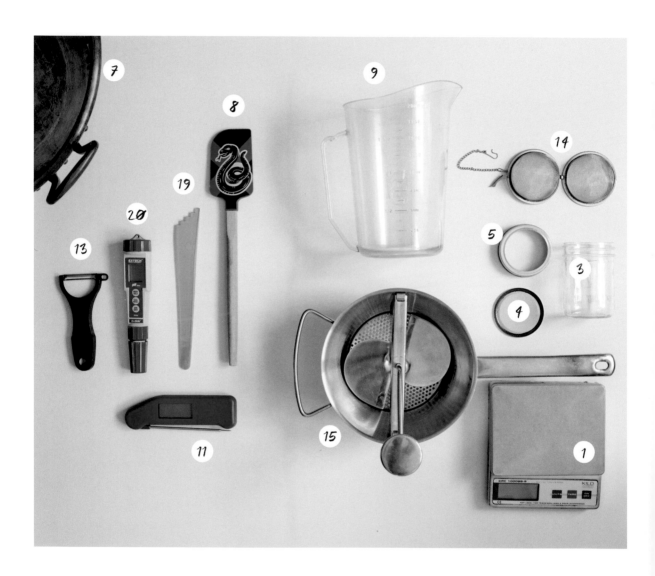

Preserving Equipment & Ingredients

First, here is the equipment you'll need, and specifics about the ingredients you'll require.

Preserving Equipment

Because I want everyone to try preserving, I like to stress that you can do it with a bare minimum of equipment. These are the essentials:

1. A Kitchen Scale This is a non-negotiable piece of equipment. Weighing prepared fruit is the only way to ensure you're using the correct amount and makes it easy to create your own recipes based on ratios. If a recipe calls for 1 kilogram of apples, everyone using a scale gets the same result. But if I say, well, I guess that's about six apples, and one person chooses a huge variety like Wolf River and another chooses tiny Lady apples and so on, there's barely any point in following a recipe—the ratios are all off!

2. A Good Knife and a Cutting Board *[not pictured]* To prep that fruit! Preferably said knife is frequently sharpened and said board is free of onion smells.

3. Jars I favor a straight-sided 250 mL (aka half-pint, 8-ounce, or 1-cup) jar, although I do get a box of diamond quilt pattern jars whenever I'm in the US. You can reuse Mason jars over and over, at least until they break or get chipped along the rim.

4. Snap Lids These are single use! Always use new snap lids. That said, I keep the used ones for all the other things I use Mason jars for—transporting smoothies, storing beans and rice, etc.

5. Ring Bands This is what holds the snap lid onto the jar. You can use them a million times, until they get rusty. Once the jars are sealed, I remove the ring bands and thread them onto a ribbon to hang somewhere until I need them again, which prevents them from rusting.

6. Quarter or Half Sheet Pans *[not pictured]* To put those jars on in the oven. Quarter sheet pans measure 9 x 13 inches (23 cm x 33 cm) and fit six jam jars perfectly. Half sheet pans measure 13 x 18 inches (33 cm x 46 cm) and are practical as cookie sheets as well.

7. A Pot Use whatever you have that is wide, heavy-bottomed, and large enough to accommodate some boiling and bubbling. You want to pick a pot with the widest circumference for the largest surface area to allow for evaporation. Don't drag out your paella pan, but avoid anything high-walled with a narrow opening.

The ideal is a copper jam pan, because copper is a great heat conductor, but I would never insist upon it, as it is pretty much just good for one thing and is quite expensive. That said, it is a lovely future heirloom that does a great job of cooking jam and makes the whole experience more beautiful—if you can afford it (and if you can, only buy one with a heavy bottom by a good brand like Mauviel). Do note that copper is reactive, so if using, make sure to mix your fruit with sugar before transferring to the copper pan to avoid the acids in the fruit causing metal to leech.

My copper pans are all very large, as they date from when I made big batches for my company, so all of the recipes in this book were tested using a 5.3-liter enameled cast iron French oven from Le Creuset that I won in a raffle.

8. Heatproof Spatula You could use a wooden spoon, but a spatula is so much more flexible and therefore better at scraping and getting in corners, thus preventing scorching. Plus its flat edge is perfect for checking sheeting (see page 24). Just make sure it's heatproof, otherwise it's going to look like a Salvador Dalí painting in about 4 minutes.

9. Ladle and/or 2-Liter Measuring Cup These will help get your jam into the jars and are just useful household items to have.

10. Oven Thermometer [*not pictured*] To make sure your oven is telling the truth and that you're actually sterilizing your jars.

11. Instant Read Thermometer Instantly verify that your jam is above 194°F (90°C) and therefore safe to can using my streamlined method. Also indispensable in baking (see page 46).

12. Stainless Steel Bowls [*not pictured*] These are lightweight, affordable (at restaurant supply stores), and what I use most often for macerating fruit with sugar. That said, glass, ceramic, or even plastic bowls will do the trick if that's what you have on hand. If macerating for a prolonged period in the fridge, a large reusable container with a lid that seals airtight is probably your best choice.

For extra credit:

13. Peeler I like a Y-shaped peeler. They are a million times easier to use than other peelers in my opinion. But you can also live dangerously like my mom and peel things with a paring knife.

14. Large Tea Ball or Small Muslin Bag This is for infusing preserves with spices, tea, coffee, herbs, or whatever else you like.

15. Food Mill A really useful tool for marmalade making to separate the juice and pulp from the seeds and membranes. That said, a mesh sieve will work in a pinch. You can also use it to make baby food, applesauce, or even mashed potatoes.

16. Blender *[not pictured]* This is essential for fruit butters and useful in a few recipes for low-pectin jams where a portion of the mixture is puréed to add body. A handheld blender or a food processor could work as well.

17. Jelly Bag or Similar *[not pictured]* This is a mesh bag for letting the juice drip off simmered fruit to make fruit juice for jelly. Personally I just use a nut milk bag (that fad didn't last long at my house, but it's a useful item nonetheless). You could also use a large sieve lined with cheesecloth.

If you're a big jelly-head and want to save time, invest in a steam juicer, which basically eliminates all the work from the recipe (you just toss the fruit in whole, unstemmed, and/or uncored) and is a same-day proposition (takes an hour!). You might get slightly less juice, but it's worth the ease of use. Just throw in a bit of extra fruit.

18. Canning Funnel *[not pictured]* This wide funnel, usually made of plastic but sometimes metal, fits perfectly into the mouth of a standard Mason jar, helping to get the jam directly into the jar with no messy spills. Because I pour most of my jams into the jar from a jug, I only use this when I'm jarring a particularly chunky preserve that doesn't pour fluidly.

19. Air Bubble Remover This little plastic stick with a notched end is very useful. The blunt end can slip in between the jar and the jam to help free any trapped air bubbles (only a problem in very chunky jams), while the notched end can sit on the rim of the jar to help you determine the correct headspace. You could also use a ruler until you're experienced enough to eyeball it.

20. PH Meter Even though almost all fruits are acidic enough to just jar up as is, if you want to create your own recipes and make certain they are safe (which is always a good idea), this will help you rest easy. A pH of 4.6 is the threshold for botulism (see page 8), so I like to make sure my preserves are below 4.0 to be sure.

That's it!!! No biggie!!!

Key Ingredients

Fruit I have a feeling you wouldn't be reading this right now if you weren't at least a little interested in seasonality. Instead of January, February, March, and so on, I could easily mark the span of year as Seville oranges, forced rhubarb, strawberries, berries, stone fruit, apples and pears, and citrus and tropical fruits. Pick the best fruit you can afford, preferably from farmers' markets, where you can talk to the growers themselves and find cool varieties grocery stores don't stock. Most of the varietals needed for my recipes can be found at your local farmers' market.

Frozen fruit is a great option for jam making. Either prepare and freeze your favorite fruits yourself in season to make jam with later on, or, out of season, use domestic frozen fruit in favor of imported fresh—the quality is usually superior. Just make sure to weigh your fruit while frozen then mix it with sugar and let it thaw before proceeding. Freezing breaks down cell walls, so if you thaw before measuring, not only are you going to have more than you likely need, the juice will have separated from the flesh and it will be a hot mess.

If you're making marmalade, you can freeze whole citrus fruits! If you're just too busy to make enough marmalade during the short Seville orange season, pop a bag of those babies in the freezer and get to it when you do have time.

Lemon Juice I prefer freshly squeezed lemon juice to bottled for its fresh flavor and lack of sulfites, which some folks are allergic to. That said, if a recipe calls for bottled lemon juice, you must use it! The acidity of lemons can vary. Bottled lemon juice is a commercial product with a constant pH, so seeing it in the ingredient list means it is vital to the acidity (and therefore safety) of a recipe.

Sugar I use your standard granulated sugar, but you can use organic cane sugar if you prefer.

For information about substituting other sweeteners or additional ingredients, see page 31.

The Streamlined Preserving Process from Start to Finish

Prepping Your Fruit

It all starts with fruit. Prepare your fruit (hull, peel, pit, whatever) if necessary before weighing.

For Jam

All my jam recipes begin with a period of maceration. This is just the prepared fruit hanging out with the sugar and lemon juice for at least 15 minutes, and up to 1 week. Cover the bowl if macerating for longer than an hour or two, and refrigerate if macerating for more than 24 hours. The sugar draws juice out of the fruit in which it dissolves, so the jam is less likely to scorch initially.

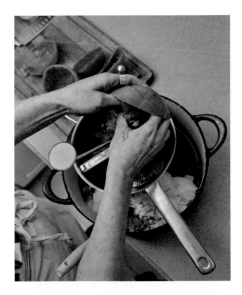

For Marmalade

My marmalade recipes are a two-step process, the first of which often requires boiling whole citrus fruits before chopping them up and mixing them with sugar for a second round of boiling. It is of the utmost importance to really nail that first step, otherwise you can end up with tough pieces of peel in your end product.

Piercing citrus fruits with the end of a wooden spoon is the classic way of checking whether they're done during the first boil. If such a blunt object can easily puncture the fruit then it must really be soft. I usually then remove the pot from the heat but let the fruit sit in it with the lid on, overnight if possible, to ensure the heat has totally penetrated the fruit, as well as allowing it to cool down (it's not fun to chop up burning hot citrus). When you cut them open to chop them up you want a total absence of white peel. It should all be translucent

and roughly the same color as the fruit. Any white peel that remains is going to stay tough once you add the sugar to the mix. Sometimes our judgment of doneness is a little off and we wind up with a few patches of white peel here and there. Just cut them out and throw them away. Then you will have perfect marmalade.

Fitting Preserving into Your Busy, Busy Life

Everyone seems to be overtaxed these days, so much so that even the thought of cooking, much less making jam or marmalade, is stressful. But I am here to tell you that by simply breaking down the process into a few easy chunks over a matter of days, even the busiest person can make homemade preserves. I want to challenge the idea that canning is an all-day affair, hot and sweaty, requiring too many pots and free time that people don't have. When I'm teaching I like to do a thought experiment . . .

Let's say you're a high-powered human rights lawyer with twelve children who does Pilates seven times a week. You only have Sunday afternoons free.

One Sunday afternoon you take your children strawberry picking to make jam later. But half of them get sunstroke! All you can manage to do is hull the strawberries listlessly and stash them in the freezer.

Three months later, you remember. You mix the frozen strawberries with sugar and lemon juice, leaving them on the counter to thaw overnight. The next day you're about to get started but you get called into an emergency board meeting! Don't worry—throw the mixture in the fridge for up to another 6 days!

Finally, you get a free afternoon and while enjoying a glass of champagne you take the 45 minutes or so of time it takes to boil that jam to a set and seal. SUCCESS!

The Streamlined Canning Process

First off, just know that if you don't feel like canning jam, you don't have to. You can just store the finished jam in the refrigerator (in jars or even in Tupperware), where it will keep for many months. But if you're anything like me, there's no room in your refrigerator. Besides which, my method is nearly as easy and doesn't take much in the way of special equipment.

There is a lot of misinformation and contradictory information about preserving floating around in the world. My canning method looks different from what you usually see in North American books. Don't freak out! I'm going to explain to you why it works. If it still makes you feel weird, no problem. You can follow the traditional instructions given on page 21 for canning fruit butters (which don't get hot enough to use this streamlined method) and heat-process all the recipes in this book for 5 minutes (adjusting for altitude if necessary). Personally, though, I don't have the time to be messing around with the big pot of boiling water that canning often demands. That's right, we're dispensing with the whole boiling jars brouhaha! Hold up, though, you can ONLY use this method for jams, jellies, and marmalades. Let me explain.

Most canning recipes require you to boil your filled jars in a pot of boiling water for a specific amount of time, which is how long it will take for the very center of the jar to attain 212°F (100°C), at which point bacteria, yeast, mold, and enzymes (see page 7) are all killed or halted. This amount of time is determined through an algorithm that takes into account the size of the jar as well as the acidity, viscosity, and initial temperature of what's inside it. This is the method you

must follow when making canned fruit (like peach halves), pickles, salsa, chutney, and all that jazz.

The thing about jam, jelly, and marmalade, though, is they get so hot that they don't need sterilizing if they go into hot sterilized jars right away.

1. Preheat your oven to 250°F (121°C). Check that your oven is truthful by using an oven thermometer, so you know its real temperature to get that safe sterilization bang on.

2. Wash your jars if they've been sitting in the basement or you just brought them home from the thrift store. I don't thoroughly wash brand new jars. I just inspect them for material contamination (broken glass, hair . . . and once I found a folded-up $5 bill!) and rinse them. If that weirds you out, though, feel free to wash them, of course. Either way, place them upside down (to avoid material contamination—just in case your oven is infested with bats!) on a cookie sheet and place them in the preheated oven at least 20 minutes before you'll need them. Keep them on the cookie sheet throughout the process so that you have a contained work area for easy cleanup and so the filled jars can be moved easily without disturbing them too much as they rest for 24 hours.

Have ring bands and new snap lids at the ready, but there's no need to prepare them in any way (unless you'd like to wash the snap lids). I know we used to heat them in hot water for 5 minutes, but I stopped doing that in 2013 after I saw a press release saying it was no longer necessary, and I've never had a problem. Besides, the lids will be sterilized by the hot jam itself.

3. When the jam is ready to be added to the jars (see page 23), turn off the heat, or turn the temperature down to low. For this method to be safe, the jam must still be above 194°F (90°C) for the entire process. Have an instant read thermometer handy to double check. Remove the baking sheet with the jars from the oven—onto a wire rack or tea towel if you're worried this might damage your countertop.

4. Fill the jars with jam to within ¼ to ⅛ inch of the rim. Use the measuring notches on the end of an air bubble remover or a regular ruler to check this if you like. The jam is hot enough that it will create a vacuum around itself and cause the jars to seal, but if they're underfilled they may not seal. I like to ladle my jam into a 2-liter (8-cup) measuring cup and pour it into the jars, using a spoon to wrangle any big pieces of fruit

if necessary, but you can also ladle it directly out of the pot and use a canning funnel to get it into the jars cleanly.

5. Wipe any jam drips off the rim with a clean wet cloth or paper towel, then screw on the lids as tightly as you can. Gardening gloves can be useful for this, as the jars are very hot, but I usually just grip the jar with a tea towel or the bottom of my apron (but it's true I have asbestos hands).

6. Invert the jars for 1 to 2 minutes, then flip right side up (otherwise the jam will set upside down) and allow to sit, undisturbed, at room temperature for 24 hours. Leaving them on the baking sheet is the easiest way to do this, but after a few hours they will be cool enough that you can transfer them to another surface if necessary.

7. Whether or not you heard the jars make that satisfying popping sound, check that they are sealed. The best way to check is to remove the ring band and then pick the jar up by the snap lid. Gravity doesn't lie! If you're feeling confident, you might also turn the jar upside down, which I call the Dairy Queen Blizzard Test. The vacuum is real. I carry jars around near and far with no ring bands and have yet to be sorry about it.

In fact, leave that ring band off when you store the jar—it will prolong the ring band's life by preventing rust, and on the off chance that something goes wrong it will be all the more apparent if the snap lid isn't being held on. Just remember to put it back on when you give away a jar as a gift—I often forget, but not everyone has a drawer full of ring bands, and seeing a jar of jam closed with an elastic band in a friend's refrigerator is so sad!

8. Put any unsealed jars in the refrigerator (it happens sometimes in spite of our best efforts). Label then store your sealed jars in a cool, dark, dry place like a cupboard, pantry, or cellar. See also A Note on Shelf Life (page 27).

The Traditional Canning Method (Necessary to Preserve Fruit Butters)

There are two fruit butters in this book (pages 132 and 145), and they need to be treated a little differently than the rest of the preserve recipes, as they don't cook in the same way and won't get quite as hot as the jams, jellies, and marmalades.

You can put them in the refrigerator straightaway, but the instructions are pretty simple for hot water bath canning them, so I encourage you to do so.

1. Preheat your oven to 250°F (121°C). At the same time, bring a large pot of water to a boil, then turn off the heat. Cover the pot so the water stays hot but not too hot (you don't want to put jars straight into rapidly boiling water, as this can cause thermal shock, breaking the jars). There should be something on the bottom of the pot to protect the jars from the hot metal—a tea towel, a silicone mat, or a perforated pizza pan that fits perfectly in the pot (that's what I use).

2. Wash your jars and place them upside down (to avoid material contamination) on a cookie sheet and place them in the preheated oven at least 20 minutes before you'll need them. Have ring bands and new snap lids at the ready.

3. When the fruit butter is ready (see page 26 for specifics about testing its set), fill the jars to within ¼ inch of the rim, then seal fingertip-tight (just until you feel resistance). This is necessary to achieve a good seal.

4. Place the jars in the pot. They must be covered by at least 1 inch of water. Replace the lid, bring to a boil on high heat, then set a timer for 10 minutes (you will need to adjust for altitude if you live on high ground—conversion charts abound online, and it's easy to search for your city's altitude as well). Turn down the heat to medium.

5. When the timer goes off, turn off the heat and remove the pot lid, and then just wait a few minutes before removing the jars to a tea towel, wooden board, or wire rack (not a marble or stainless steel countertop, once again to avoid thermal shock), then proceed as above for checking the seals and storing.

The Greatest Feat: How to Tell if Your Jam Is Ready

Allow me to begin with a cautionary tale.

One of my former assistants once worked at a not-so-great bakery. One day, on entering the basement kitchen, she smelled the telltale signs of something gone awry and exclaimed, "Something's burning!"

The pastry chef, not even bothering to turn around, replied imperiously, "I'm making strawberry jam."

"Well, it's burning," she countered.

"No, it's not done. It has yet to reach 220 degrees."

At that she capitulated to her misguided superior.

The jam was, of course, burnt, but she was made to pass it in cakes all week anyway!

This is why I would never use a thermometer to judge whether or not a jam is done. So often when we have a tool of measurement like a thermometer, or a specific number we are seeking, we become so fixated on it that we cease to register the goings-on of the physical world, like the smell of burning jam. Far too often I get students in class telling stories of jams that were so overcooked they couldn't get them out of the jar, and nearly always those students had cooked the jam to a specified temperature.

Of course, thermometers are wonderful tools. Don't get me wrong. Once the jam is done, they are necessary to verify it stays above a minimum temperature for safe canning. And they are perfect for making caramel, for instance—a recipe in which all the ingredients have a pretty standardized amount of water and fat, and which is very high in sugar.

Fruit, on the other hand, is mercurial. It changes from one day to the next. On a rainy day, strawberries will have absorbed plenty more water than if they were picked after a week without. If you're making jam in which there is nearly as much (or more!) sugar than fruit, you can judge it by its temperature, as if you were making candy. But with a lower-sugar jam, that method is folly.

What's more, there's merit in taking the time to observe the jam, to hone your skills of observation. I like to tell my students that jam making is as good for you, as relaxing, as meditation or yoga. It requires you to be present, observing the transformation of physical matter.

Of course, there is a tool producers use to tell if their jam is ready. It's called a refractometer, and it measures the concentration of sugar. You don't need one.

Knowing when your jam is done is the most difficult part of making jam. Mostly, it just takes observation and practice. Don't be discouraged if ever you don't get the right set. As Julia Child said, "No one is born a great cook, one learns by doing." Just learn from your mistakes and make some more jam! However, it is better to err on the side of undercooking than overcooking. If you've undercooked your jam, you can just empty it back into the pot and cook it some more (using new lids, of course), whereas you have no recourse with overcooked jam other than to try to convince someone you made pâte de fruits.

How to Tell if Your Jam Is Done, per the Five Senses (in Order of Importance)

Observe! You need to know how it looks at the beginning to know how it's changed, indicating it's ready, so pay attention the whole time.

Sight

- Bubbles will change from frothy and chaotic into large, blinking fish eyes.
- The surface will become glossy and jewel-like, absorbing any foam that was present (except in the case of very foamy jams, like apricot and strawberry—they need a little skimming).
- Check the sheeting (see next section).

Sound

- The initial white noise will become rhythmic, like something you could almost dance to.
- When you pull your spatula through, it will sound like a slavering ogre.

Touch

- When you pull your spatula through, it will change from its initial easy gliding to feeling as though a hidden sea monster is trying to wrestle it from you.
- Some jams will begin to spit and burn you—watch out!

Smell

- Not actually that useful, as it's very hard to describe how the smell changes when a jam is ready, but I swear it does.

Taste

- Don't taste it—it's too hot!

On Sheeting

I use all of my senses (besides taste), as described above, to determine if the jam is done, but sheeting is the most telling sign. Sheeting refers to how the jam slowly drips off a spatula when lifted to eye level. When the jam clings to the spatula, drops join together, or, in more pectin-rich jam, it falls in clumps or sheets, it's ready.

A note on form: Often I see folks attempt to check the sheeting by removing the spatula only an inch or so above the bubbling pot, where they can scarcely see it and where it will never cool down enough to give a good idea of the final texture. I encourage everyone to be proud and hoist that spatula up to eye level. You will not only look confident, but also be far more able to confidently assess the set.

To add drama, I tell my students to imagine this as a love story, wherein we are looking for the jam to fall in love with the spatula. At first, the mixture will sluice off, falling like rain. I liken this to an interested glance through a foggy bus window, or an introduction at work. Later, when the jam begins to coat the spatula and hesitate a little before succumbing to gravity, you have a tête-à-tête at a wine bar. A single drop that lingers stubbornly is a sweater the jam leaves

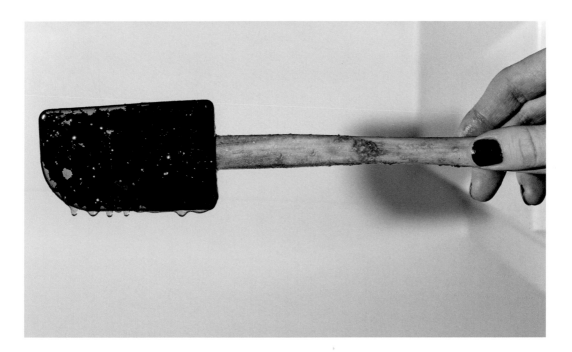

at the spatula's house so that it will think of them once they leave. You get the idea. What we really want, though, is for the jam to declare undying love for the spatula, clinging to it fiercely and declaring wild horses will never tear them apart! You are in no way obligated to use the same metaphor, but I think having one makes it all a little more exciting.

Your Best Insurance: The Freezer Plate Test

The fact is, it takes a lot of practice to be able to judge a jam's set just by observing it cook. Fortunately, there's an easy test with a very low failure rate you can do. It's called the freezer plate test.

1. Before you start your project, put a small plate or two in your freezer. When I first started making jam in earnest, I would always have a few in there so I'd never be caught out.

2. When you think the jam is done, remove it from the heat (you can always cook it more if it's not done yet, but you can never turn back time and uncook it) and put a teaspoon of it onto one of the cold plates.

3. Return the plate to the freezer and wait 2 minutes. If you had to use a room-temperature plate because you forgot to freeze one, just leave it in for an extra 30 to 45 seconds.

4. Remove the plate from the freezer and give the lump of jam a gentle nudge with your finger. If it has formed a skin and wrinkles like a silk robe on the deck of Harry Styles's yacht, it's ready. If not, keep cooking and try again in a few minutes.

5. Extra credit: Run your finger right through the jam on the plate, parting it like the Red Sea. If the line stays and the jam doesn't creep right back to fill it in, it's definitely ready. I call this the Moses Test.

But What About Fruit Butters?

It's true that checking the set on fruit butter is a little different than for jam, jelly, and marmalade. Fruit butters may form a skin if you do the freezer plate test, but most of all we want to check that they hold their shape and that enough water has evaporated from the mixture.

To check the set of a fruit butter, put a spoonful on a plate and wait a few minutes. If the fruit butter slumps and spreads, it's not done. We want it to sit in a stoic mound, like a mountain. As well, look at its edges. When enough water has yet to evaporate, a ring of transparent liquid will form around it. When this ring is absent or just razor thin, it's done.

A Note on Shelf Life

My friend Kinneret called me one day about 13 months after we'd canned some applesauce together. She had seen it was more than a year old and was poised by the edge of the sink, ready to throw it out. "Hey," she said. "Can I eat this?"

"If it tastes good, then sure," I replied. It did and she did. Happy ending.

Because of botulism (see page 7), canning can have a general air of danger for many people, so they consider the recommended shelf life of a year for a jar of preserves to be a hard line. Like most best before dates, however, jam's is just that—a guess about what will be the prime time during which to eat it, not a deadline after which it turns deadly.

I do have a vague system for managing the age of my preserves, trying to rotate the oldest to the front of my pantry so they get eaten first, but I also live with someone who likes to root around to find red berry jam no matter what other flavors are languishing on the frontlines. Do your best.

With time, the taste, texture, and color of preserves slowly start to degrade (though storing them properly will certainly help mitigate this). But just like I'm known to use buttermilk long past its expiration date, I find jams that are a few months to a year past their prime are often still perfectly delicious, if a little faded in color.

The one exception to this rule is marmalade, which many people believe improves with age. I particularly like Seville marmalade once it's at least a year old: the texture thickens, the color darkens, and the flavor becomes even richer. Apparently a jar of marmalade that was found with the remains of some explorers who had disappeared (and evidently died) 25 years prior was found to be "positively ambrosial."

Take these steps to make sure you enjoy your preserves at their best:

1. Label! It sounds obvious, but I used to always think I'd remember what everything was, then find myself squinting at a jar of red jam months later, trying to ascertain its flavor based on the presence of seeds. Now I write what it is and when I made it, usually on a piece of green painter's tape affixed to the jar— not beautiful, but certainly practical. Restaurant habits die hard.

2. Store your preserves somewhere cool, dark, and dry. Do your best, but just definitely don't keep them somewhere like the dashboard of your car or in a bucket of water.

3. Rotate your preserves so you don't misplace things and let them get old and sad.

Creativity: Crafting Your Own Jam from Alpha to Omega

Suppose you find some fruits in season or on sale, and you want to turn them into a lovely jam but I haven't given you a recipe for it here. Or, suppose after cooking your way through all the preserve recipes in this book you want to spread your wings and invent your own flavor concoctions. Fortunately, the process is just about the same no matter what fruit you use. And because fruit is acidic, it's perfectly safe to invent your own recipes, as long as you *do not add* any basic (alkaline) ingredients (such as baking soda or alkalized cocoa powder) and *always add* lemon juice. You're going to have to do a little math, but everyone's got a calculator now, so no biggie.

To reiterate, you can only do this with jam, jelly, and marmalade recipes, because fruit is acidic. As I said earlier, though, if you want to buy a pH meter to make certain your recipes are safe, go ahead! Or use a pre-existing recipe from a trusted source and just change the sugar proportions, sweetener, or flavorings.

Avoid creating your own jams with any of the following fruit, which hover too near the upper limit of pH for safe acidity: bananas, papayas, melon, white peaches, ripe mango, Asian pears, and figs. Instead, use a recipe from a trusted source for these.

A Basic Jam Recipe to Get You Started

Makes four to six 250 mL (8 oz) jars (depending on the fruit)

1 kg (2 lb + 3 oz) prepared fruit
500–650 g (2½–3¼ cups) sugar
45 mL (3 Tbsp) lemon juice
Additional flavorings (optional)

In a large bowl, combine the fruit, sugar, and lemon juice and let macerate, for at least 15 minutes, or up to 1 week, covered in the refrigerator.

Prepare the jars (see page 20).

Transfer the mixture to a pot or preserving pan. Heat on medium-high and bring to a hard boil, stirring frequently.

When the setting point is reached (see page 23), remove from the heat and pour into prepared jars to within ¼ to ⅛ inch of the rim. Remove any air bubbles, wipe the rims if necessary, seal, and invert for 1 to 2 minutes. Flip right side up and let the jam sit, undisturbed, for 24 hours.

 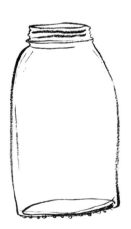  

Fruit It all starts with fruit. Ideally, you want a mixture of 75% perfectly ripe and 25% slightly underripe fruit, since the riper fruit gets, the less pectin it contains. It might feel weird to use a partially white strawberry or a hard apricot, but they will disappear into the mix and give you a better set.

Prepare your fruit (hull, peel, pit, whatever) before weighing it. You can use frozen fruit in the same weight as well (see page 16). Either way, you want a maximum of 2 kilograms (4 pounds + 6 ounces) net, keeping in mind a smaller amount will be easier to manage. Larger amounts take exponentially longer amounts of time to cook and are easier to burn and misjudge the set. If you need to make a lot of jam, make multiple batches instead of one big one.

Sugar In time you will find your own ratio, but mine is 50% for sweeter fruits like strawberries and peaches, and up to 65% for more acidic fruits like rhubarb and currants (see the table on page 33). (I used to add less sugar [30% to 50%], but ended up increasing my percentages a little to get a better shelf life

and easier set.) This means that for every kilogram (2 pounds + 3 ounces) of fruit I have, I add 500 grams to 650 grams (2½ cups to 3¼ cups) of sugar.

If I'm combining two fruits with different acidities, I separately calculate the amount of sugar for the weight of each, according to their percentages, before adding them together.

You might also want to substitute some or all of the sugar. Usually I start by substituting half the amount with a different sweetener, then see if I want to take it further next time. Substitute brown sugar, honey, or maple sugar gram for gram with white sugar. (Substituting gram for gram instead of cup for cup is essential for sweeteners like honey, which are both sweeter and heavier than sugar. If you go cup for cup you'll end up with a much sweeter jam.) Just remember, a 100% honey-sweetened jam will have a shorter shelf life once it's open (see page 27).

Lemon Juice I add 45 mL (3 tablespoons) of lemon juice, which is about equivalent to the juice of one lemon, for every kilogram (2 pounds + 3 ounces) of fruit. Double that for marmalade. Not only

does the lemon juice increase acidity and offset a little of the sugar, but it also activates the natural pectin in fruit.

Additional Flavorings Throw some more flavor on! Here are some things you might want to add. Note that some ingredients will need to be added before you bring the mixture to a hard boil, others will need to be added after it has just reached a boil, and some only once it's off the heat. I have noted these throughout.

Herbs Hardy herbs like fresh rosemary, thyme, and lavender can go straight into the pot or be put in a tea ball to infuse for easy removal. Be cautious with these though—they are very strong and a little goes a long way!

Softer herbs like fresh mint and basil leaves can be added at the very end of cooking so they don't get destroyed by the heat. Another great option is to grind these herbs with some of the sugar and add it with the rest of the sugar to really release the oils.

Spices I love adding whole spices like star anise straight into the pot, but grinding spices or putting them into a tea ball to infuse is a good move too. Make sure they are relatively fresh for maximum effect.

Booze I often use liqueurs to add flavor to preserves because they are distillates and so they have a really strong, pure flavor. Sometimes it's nice to match the liqueur to the fruit, like adding Poire William to pear jam, just to amplify the flavor that's already there, but you can also get more creative. Add these once the jam is ready and off the heat to prevent all of the alcohol from volatizing (it will still mostly volatize when you add it to hot jam off the heat, but more of the flavor will remain intact without prolonged boiling).

When you're adding less-concentrated alcohol like beer or wine, reduce it first by boiling it until it's about one-third of the original volume. This way you aren't adding any extra water to your mixture.

Tea and Coffee Again, because you don't want to add extra water, infuse tea leaves or coffee beans directly into your boiling jam by using a tea ball.

Dried Fruit Raisins, dried apricots, sour cherries, golden berries—they can all be excellent additions. Mix them in during the maceration stage, or plump them in alcohol or juice first.

Nuts These can add great flavor and texture, but I advise against toasting them first, which can enhance their flavor so much that it takes over. Add once the mixture comes to a boil.

Cocoa Nibs These are hands down the best way to add chocolate flavor to a jam without disrupting the acidity, adding sugar, or having to emulsify any fats. You get a burst of chocolate flavor and a cool polka-dot look. Add once the mixture comes to a boil.

Other Flavorings Rose water, orange flower water, vanilla, elderflower syrup . . . All sorts of extracts can be interesting additions. Add these delicate additions once the jam is ready and off the heat.

Acid When you cook fruit, its vibrant fresh acidity disappears. If you want your jam to have a fresher fruit flavor, a little citric acid does wonders. A splash of vinegar can also be interesting, especially if it's fruit-flavored. Add these once the jam is ready and off the heat.

Choose Your Own Adventure

Of course, everyone has their own specific tastes and proclivities, but this is how I would sweeten these common jam fruits and what I might pair with them.

Fruit	Sugar (g per kg of fruit)	Pectin Level	Plays Well With
Apricot	50% (500 g/kg)	Low	Almonds, chamomile, honey, orange flower water, pistachios, raspberries
Blueberry	50% (500 g/kg)	Low	Blackberries, coffee, gin, lavender, lemon, lime, thyme, violets
Peach	50% (500 g/kg)	Low	Bourbon, cinnamon, fig leaf, honey, Muscat, white currants
Plum	50% (500 g/kg)★ ★depending on variety—high acid damsons I sweeten at 66%	High	Black pepper, caramelized sugar, cinnamon, grappa, orange, star anise
Raspberry	55% (550 g/kg)	Medium	Candied citrus peel, cocoa nib, figs, fruit vinegar, lime, plums, star anise
Rhubarb	66% (660 g/kg)	Low	Angelica, cardamom, cherries (sweet/sour/fresh/dried), kumquat, Seville orange, vanilla
Strawberry	50% (500 g/kg)	Low	Chamomile, lemon, lemon balm, red currants, rhubarb, rosé wine, vanilla

A Guide to Buying Quality Jam

You may find you are short on time, missed out on local apricots during their short season, or simply aren't in the mood to make jam. Although I really wish you would make jam and strongly encourage you to do so, there are times where you will likely want to buy some jam or marmalade. Here are some things to keep in mind when buying your next preserve.

Quality Jam Is Worth the Price The fact is, high-quality jams and marmalades are going to be more expensive than their lower-quality counterparts. They have to be. Higher-quality fruit, smaller batches, and hopefully better wages for the people growing, harvesting, and transforming the fruit all contribute to a higher cost, but it's worth it.

Buy from Your Local Farmers' Market or Craft Fairs . . . Farmers' markets and craft fairs often have excellent jams that taste more homemade than industrial, and they are likely made with local fruit (perhaps even grown by the jam maker themselves). Artisanal preservers make jam in smaller batches using methods closer to the ones outlined in this book and often offer more creative flavor combinations (although some will follow old-fashioned recipes that contain much more sugar than I like). Besides, choosing jam is usually easier at a farmers' market or craft fair because the vendors will let you taste their various offerings. Just try them and buy the one you like! And you can support your local economy too.

But Those Imported Preserves Made with Uncommon Fruits Can Be Wonderful Too I usually prefer to buy preserves made with local ingredients, but if you're on the hunt for a fruit or flavor that's unusual in your part of the world, imported products are wonderful. You are often more likely, for example, to find a good damson jam or Seville marmalade imported from England than from your area. Visit a specialty food store that stocks products from the parts of the world where your desired flavors flourish.

Don't Judge a Jam by Its Pretty Label It can be overwhelming to be confronted with a vast selection of sealed jars in a shop. You could just pick one based on the label, like I used to do with wine in my 20s. However, while a good label may indicate a commitment to excellence in every area, including marketing, or it could just as equally be designed to disguise an inferior product, while a bad label could be down to a producer who cares much more about the jam being good than spending money on design.

Read the Label Since definitions of preserves can vary so widely, the ingredient label offers much more information than the name of the product does. If sugar is the first ingredient listed, it is generally not a good sign for jam. Marmalade, on the other hand, requires a higher volume of sugar to balance the bitterness of the citrus peel, so it's perfectly normal to see it listed at the top. Also, steer clear of preserves made from high-pectin fruit (such as citrus, currants, crabapples, or cranberries) with added pectin. Pectin in this case was likely added to increase yield rather than taste, and there's no need for it there at all! That said, pectin isn't always to be avoided in other jams—it's hard to make larger volumes of low-pectin fruit into jam without using some. Lastly,

avoid products that contain additional preservatives to increase shelf life, such as sodium benzoate and potassium sorbate.

When you're reading the fine print, be aware that the terminology can be misleading. Moreover, the laws and definitions required vary from country to country, further complicating matters. Jam and marmalade often have legal definitions that indicate the concentration of sugar they must contain (which to my taste is generally very high, depending on the fruit). On the other hand, "fruit spread" often indicates a lower-sugar product, but it isn't a legally protected term like jam, so that won't necessarily be the case. When in doubt, defer to the ingredient list or, in a perfect world, talk directly to the jam maker!

Baking 101

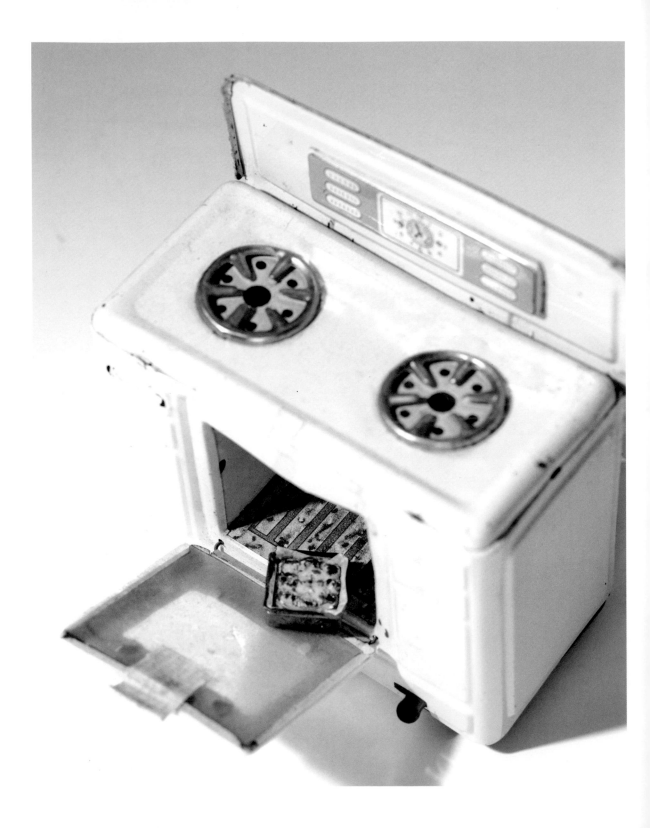

Baking Is All About the World Observed

Baking is completely intimidating to some people, and as natural as breathing to others. Either way, you can always improve your skills and improve your day by making something sweet.

Baking Is Relaxing, and Yes, Practice Makes Perfect

Bakers are thought of as rigid and scientific, but this isn't really accurate and also dichotomizes baking and cooking. While it's true that you shouldn't dramatically change the quantities in a given recipe if you want it to turn out (it is chemistry, after all), much of baking is still about the feeling. It's knowing a texture, a look. Testing if a steak is done by touching it, as chefs do, isn't really different from checking if croissant dough is ready for its next turn by giving it a poke. That's why so many grannies just eyeball their pie dough yet still consistently make the best pie you've ever had.

Home-baking shouldn't be stressful. As with learning to make perfectly set jam, it's all about practice. The more you repeat a task, the more it sinks in, becomes second nature, and, if you're paying attention, you'll begin to understand what works and why. If you don't nail something the first time, don't be hard on yourself. Just make it again when

you next have free time, and relish the peaceful routine of kneading dough, creaming butter, separating eggs . . .

Here are some things I have learned along the way as a teacher, pastry chef, and home cook.

1. Read the whole recipe through before beginning, a few days before if possible. So many times I've made this mistake and suddenly the cake I was going to make for that evening's dinner party was a no-go because I should have started it 2 days earlier.

2. Mise-en-place is key. It's French for basically having everything in place. You don't need all your ingredients laid out in tiny bowls like on a cooking show, but make sure you have everything you need in sufficient quantity close at hand. I bake so much and buy ingredients in such large quantities that I always assume I have everything I need, but that can lead me to sometimes freak out in the middle of a recipe when it turns out I don't actually have a can of evaporated milk or a cup of flaked coconut.

3. Have your ingredients at the right temperature. This is like a subset of mise-en-place. For the most part with baking ingredients, like likes like. If you're making pie dough, you want all your ingredients to be refrigerator-cold, if not colder. On the other hand, when you're making cake, a refrigerator-cold egg can cause soft butter to seize up and curdle the mixture. If you forget to temper anything, fast fixes can help—like microwaving butter in short bursts to soften it, or warming eggs in a bowl of hot tap water. Don't worry, though—I specify temperatures in each recipe when it's important.

4. WEIGH YOUR INGREDIENTS!!!

Using a kitchen scale for baking is becoming more and more common in North America, but just in case you have yet to convert, let me give you the hard sell: Ten people could all measure a cup of flour. But each of those cups could weigh wildly different amounts, since some people pack it in, while others have a lighter touch. This could lead to some dry, crumbly cakes at one extreme and wet, sticky ones at the other. If we all just agree that 1 cup of flour weighs 140 grams, we can all make perfect cakes and get on with our lives. (You may notice not every baker or publication agrees that 1 cup of flour weighs 140 grams, but this has been my rule of thumb for almost 20 years, so I am committed.)

I don't, however, weigh small amounts that I could measure with measuring spoons. Most affordable kitchen scales just aren't that accurate. We used to use a jeweler's scale (purchased at a head shop!) for small amounts of things like agar-agar at restaurants where

I worked, but we're not doing molecular gastronomy here, so for amounts of 2 tablespoons or less, you'll see only the volume amount listed.

The added bonus of using a scale is not having to scrape out or clean measuring cups! You're welcome.

However, not to be exclusionary, I have included cup measurements (and approximate numbers of fruits, if required), but I still believe that the recipes will only come out perfectly if weighed.

5. Baking and cooking times are not written in stone.

We are not baking in the same oven on the same day, so while I've tried hard to be accurate about times in these recipes, they may not be quite the same for you in your circumstances (Thinner baking sheets! Lighter-colored pan! Who knows?!). Always trust your senses rather than adhering strictly to the times given, instead focusing on the sensory descriptions of what the thing should look like when it's done. An instant read thermometer will go a long way in assuring accuracy as well.

6. Make yeast work for you.

Historically I've never been big on yeasted treats simply because if I wanted to serve them for, say, brunch, all that rising required *me* to rise at an unholy hour. The ultimate life hack is to own a proofer, like I would use at work, but that's unreasonable. Instead, remember that at any point you can raise dough in the refrigerator overnight instead of for an hour or two at room temperature. I find it easiest to make the dough after supper, let it do a first rise while I curl up with a book and a glass of sherry, then before bed just portion and shape the dough (the work of mere minutes!) and put it in the refrigerator (hopefully you have room!). The next morning, just pull it out and let it come to room temperature before baking.

7. Use your hands. Yes, your hands are really one of your best tools in baking. As long as you remember to wash them frequently, there's no better way to check if sugar is dissolved in Swiss meringue, make an angel food cake, pit damsons, mash strawberries, or break up big butter clumps in galette dough.

8. Save your scraps. I'm of two minds about including this, seeing as I tend to save so many sundry items that I can never realistically get around to using them. I'll just remind you that scraps of sweet tart dough or sablé Breton dough make excellent cookies to tuck into lunch boxes, as do scraps of pie dough twisted up with cinnamon sugar and baked until golden. Extra egg whites or yolks are just a good excuse to make custard or pavlova, and citrus peel should be candied. In fact, even apple peels should sometimes be candied. Excess chocolate glaze makes a great ice cream sauce. You get the idea. Let's throw out less food.

9. Supreme your citrus. Citrus supremes are segments of fruit denuded of peel, pith, and membrane, like canned mandarin oranges. I just read that supremes are so 1990s and that citrus wheels are what's up in the 2020s, but I pay no heed to trends (or at least try not to). Fact is, both are good, but I do slightly favor a supreme, which dispenses entirely of the membranes to expose all of those beautiful little juice vesicles clinging together. It's not hard; it just takes practice.

- Cut a bit off either end of your citrus fruit so a little of the flesh is exposed. Place on a cutting board and use a small serrated or paring knife to remove the skin and membrane, taking it off in swaths starting at the top, then following the curve of the fruit down to the bottom. You may have to trim off a little more pith once all the peel is gone (and save that peel to candy it).

- Holding the denuded fruit over a bowl, cut between the membranes and the flesh of each section. Once I have the first piece out, I usually just cut down one side, then turn my knife under and flip out the section with it, which should come cleanly off the membrane on that side, no cutting necessary. I like to give the empty membranes a squeeze once all the segments are out to get any last drops of juice out, because the juice drained off the supremes is the cook's treat!

10. Bake with jam! Obviously, that's what this book is about. But to go beyond using jam as just a filling, try thinking about it as a liquid sweetener. Try substituting honey or corn syrup with jam or jelly. In recipes that call for candied citrus peel, use marmalade instead (just keep in mind you may have to dial back the liquid in the recipe a little). Experiment!

11. Bake with whatever else you want! Creativity really is my life force, so I totally understand if you want to put your own spin on things. As much as I love recipes, I also love modifying them to suit my tastes or to try out a hunch. While I don't recommend drastically altering proportions, substituting different nuts, liqueurs, or other flavorings is highly encouraged. If you like alternative flours, you can usually substitute up to half the flour in a recipe for another. Get weird!

Baking Equipment & Star Ingredients

Just as I want everyone to be making jam, I also want everyone to be baking. To that end, I think you can get started with whatever equipment you have in your cupboards right now. I do realize that the majority of people don't have all the baking equipment in their home that I do. Why would they? That said, if you are an avid baker or have dreams of becoming one, I've made a list here of the items I think are indispensable.

I highly recommend buying the majority of your equipment in a restaurant supply store. The items you'll find there are made to last—to stand up to a great amount of abuse, in fact—and are generally cheaper than you'll find elsewhere. That said, any local kitchenware store should have everything you need, or there's always the Internet. I remember being shocked in pastry school when a number of things we had to buy for our kits came from the hardware store!

Necessary or Useful Equipment

1. Parchment Paper *[not pictured]* If you're not already using this nonstick paper to line pans, know that it will change your life. It is indispensable in baking. For lining cookie sheets, silicone mats, such as Silpats, are wonderful and reusable as well, but you'll still need parchment to line cake pans and the like.

2. Plastic Wrap *[not pictured]* I wish I didn't have to include this, but in a lot of cases there isn't a viable alternative. It's essential for tightly wrapping dough that might otherwise dry out, preventing custards from forming a skin, lining molds for easy and clean removal of gelée or nougat glacé . . .

3. Heatproof Spatula(s) A flexible and non-melting essential.

4. Whisk(s) Ideally a full-size one as well as a baby one for things like egg wash (though you can use a fork if necessary).

5. Stainless Steel Bowls *[not pictured]* These are cheap, light, sturdy, and heatproof (hello, double boiler), and they nest for easy storage.

6. Baking Pans I prefer uncoated, light-colored metal pans with straight sides and sharp corners. The essentials are:

- 12-cup muffin tin
- 8-inch square pan
- 5- x 9-inch loaf pan
- Half sheet pans
- 10- x 15-inch jelly roll pan

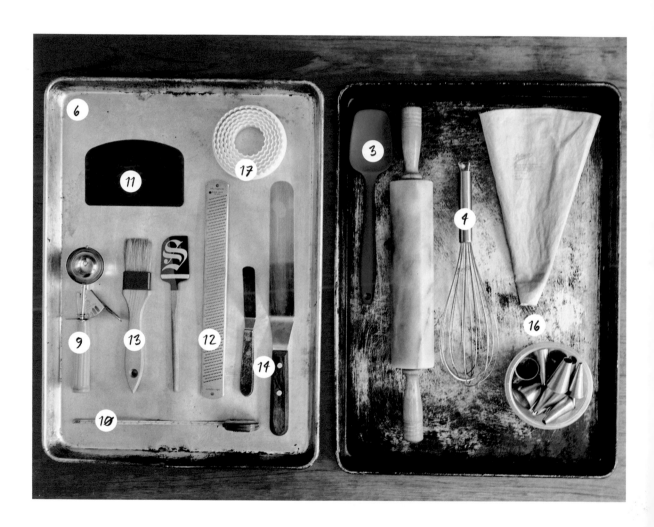

- Tube pan (preferably with a removable bottom, also known as an angel food cake pan)
- Bundt pan
- Two 6-inch round cake pans
- 8½-inch springform pan
- 9-inch tart pan with removable bottom

7. Wire Cooling Rack *[not pictured]* Having one of these means you won't be putting a hot pan straight onto your countertop or precariously balancing it on two oven mitts. It will let the air circulate, meaning the pan cools down faster and eliminates prolonged exposure to heat once you've achieved a perfect bake. It's also very helpful when you're glazing cakes.

8. Ramekins *[not pictured]* I have a few sets of ramekins, and they're great for making panna cotta and crème brûlée, baking individual cakes, and serving olives. But you can always make do with wide-mouth 250 mL (8-ounce) jars, since you're hopefully making jam anyway.

9. Ice Cream Scoops These are perfect for portioning out cookie dough. This is the secret to how bakery cookies look so good. They also are great for scooping, duh, ice cream.

10. Measuring Tape or Ruler Measuring comes up a lot in pastry, whether it's dimensions for rolling out dough or making sure you've got the right size of pan. Always have a measuring tape (or ruler) nearby. Mine is a refrigerator magnet, which makes it a no-brainer (unless, of course, you have a stainless steel refrigerator . . .).

11. Dough Scraper This flat piece of plastic is excellent for scraping bowls, portioning dough, decorating cakes, cleaning surfaces of flour and dough—a bargain for one dollar or two!

12. Microplane Grating zest, ginger, and nutmeg has never been easier.

13. Pastry Brushes These are pretty essential for brushing on egg wash, glazes, and the like. Have two or three different sizes, all with natural bristles.

14. Offset Spatulas These little guys are indispensable for all the spreading of jams, batters, glazes, and icings bakers do. Get a large one and a mini one to handle any task.

15. Fine Mesh Sieve *[not pictured]* For sifting dry ingredients or straining lumps out of creams and custards.

16. Piping Bag and Assorted Tips In no way essential, but pretty fun to play around with.

17. Set of Round Cutters I remember not really getting how these could be useful when my grandmother gave me a set as a gift, but 20 years later I still have the same set and it has proved indispensable. You'll need these for cutting out rolled cookies, tart shells, donuts . . . the list goes on.

18. Instant Read Thermometer *[not pictured]* I love my thermometer so much, even if I won't use it to check the set of jam. Not only is it essential for making things like candy and Italian meringue, it's also the best way to check whether your baked goods are done. When the thermometer reads 210°F (99°C), you're good to go, no subjective contemplation of a toothpick's crumb cling necessary.

19. Blowtorch *[not pictured]* If you like crème brûlée or lemon meringue pie, this is a must. Sure, you can put either of them under the broiler in your oven, but the result will not be as even. A blowtorch gives you total control and looks cool, and you can use it to fix frozen pipes in the winter if you live in Montreal. It's actually very useful if you have a stand mixer but not a microwave to soften butter or temper buttercream (just mix on medium-low while applying some fire to the outside of the bowl!).

I have no time for fiddly little kitchen torches. A propane torch from the hardware store is cheaper

and more powerful, although I do prefer the slightly fancier ones with the self-lighting heads.

20. Ice Cream Maker *[not pictured]* Essential if you want to make ice cream, but if you don't have one you can still make delicious, creamy frozen treats such as Chocolate-Speckled Ice Cream (page 58).

21. Microwave *[not pictured]* This is a secret weapon in a baker's kitchen, perfect for tempering butter in 15-second bursts when you forgot to leave it out or have a last-minute baking craving. It makes melting and even tempering chocolate so much easier. Just make sure to melt chocolate in 20- to 30-second increments, stirring between bursts, to prevent scorching.

22. Stand Mixer *[not pictured]* I'm not about to tell you this pricey item is a must, but if you love baking it will be your best friend, so consider saving up or begging someone for one. My father surprised me with a KitchenAid Pro almost 20 years ago when he got a tax refund from my education credits, and it's still going strong. Best gift ever.

That said, if you can't afford one or just don't bake enough for it to be worth it, almost any of the recipes in this book that reference using a stand mixer can be pulled off using an electric handheld mixer or just some good old-fashioned elbow grease. If I'm whipping a cup of cream or less, or just a few egg whites, I'll often just do it by hand even though I have a mixer.

Key Baking Ingredients

When you source your baking ingredients for all of these recipes, here are some things to keep in mind/strong opinions I have.

Butter Unsalted, always. I don't usually splurge on the higher-fat stuff unless I'm baking something where butter is the star of the flavor show (but I probably would if I could afford it). I always have a few blocks of butter in my freezer in case of emergency (or when there's been a sale).

Chocolate While I don't think you should be blowing half a paycheck on baking chocolate, the quality of the chocolate you use really determines how good your baking will be. I use chocolate pistoles (or callets, or feves, or wafers, or disks—they have many names), which are different from chocolate chips in that they contain more cocoa butter and usually less sugar. While Valrhona is my preferred brand, I tested the recipes in this book using a less costly one containing 75% cocoa solids for the dark chocolate and 40% for the milk.

Cocoa Powder As with chocolate, the better the cocoa powder you use, the better your finished product will be. I use an extra-dark alkalized (aka Dutch process) cocoa powder that gives a lot of bang for your buck.

Eggs Always large; free-range if possible. Weigh them if the recipe calls for large quantities. A large egg should weigh about 50 grams, 20 grams of which is yolk and 30 grams white.

Flours All-purpose flour is truly versatile, as the name suggests, but it's a shame that it's almost totally taken over, since there is such a wealth of different grains in the world. I love to use all sorts of flour, many that aren't wheat. They aren't always easy to find, but they will holistically improve your life if you're able to track them down. Many areas have local mills that produce many other types of flour than white and whole wheat that are fresher and often more nutritious than the standard grocery store fare.

I like to use kamut flour (aka khorasan) when I'm baking with citrus because of its golden color, sort of like treating baking as a matching game. I like to use rye flour in recipes with coffee or whisky, maybe because it's used in whisky and whisky is good in coffee? But mostly because they taste good together. Buckwheat pairs well with chocolate, and so on. Experiment with alternatives (just substitute in a portion of the total weight of flour)!

Gelatin I prefer sheet gelatin to powdered by about a billion percent. I probably haven't used the powdered stuff in over a decade, if not longer. Sheet gelatin is far, far easier to use. You simply count (and weigh to be accurate: 1 sheet = 2 grams) the sheets, soak them in cold water for a few minutes, then squeeze them out before stirring them into hot liquid, where they dissolve completely.

Sheet gelatin is not as readily available as powdered, but it's easy to find online. If you want to use powdered, however, use this formula:

5 sheets gelatin = 1 envelope powdered gelatin (7 grams/2½ teaspoons)

Lard Lard is a great fat for things like pie crusts. If you can, get it at a butcher shop or deli that renders it on site—the flavor will be far superior to that of lard from the supermarket shelf. If you're vegetarian, feel free to replace it with vegetable shortening or butter.

Nuts Buy nuts in small quantities, or store them in the refrigerator or freezer, as it is a serious bummer to tuck into a delicious baked good only to fall upon a rancid nut.

To toast nuts, spread them onto a baking sheet and bake at 350°F (175°C) for about 10 minutes, until fragrant and tanned.

I can easily find ground almonds and hazelnuts where I live, but if you can't, grind the nuts in a food processor with some of the sugar from the recipe, just taking care not to go too far (or you'll end up with nut butter).

Oil I generally use grapeseed oil for its neutral flavor and high smoke point, but you can use whatever neutral oil you have on hand—canola, vegetable, sunflower . . .

Salt Whenever a recipe calls for salt, with no other description, I used Diamond Kosher Salt. That means that if you're using a finer salt, you might end up with a little more than I did, since it's measured by volume. This shouldn't be a problem, since the quantities are generally so small, but it's good to know if you want to start doubling or tripling recipes.

When I call for flaky salt, I used Maldon salt, pyramid-shaped salt crystals from England, but you could use fleur de sel or anything else similar. I use flaky salt for finishing dishes and adding crunch to the tops of baked goods.

Vanilla I often go off on a tangent when I'm teaching about the fascinating reasons for vanilla's huge price inflation in recent years. Google it! I still use costly vanilla beans when vanilla is the star of the flavor show, but I stretch my dollar by rinsing and drying the used beans then either steeping them in brandy to make my own vanilla extract (haven't bought that stuff in years!) or in sugar to make vanilla sugar (excellent to have on hand). When I want a little extra vanilla pop and those pretty black dots but don't want to spring for a bean, I use vanilla paste. If substituting vanilla paste for a vanilla bean, use 1 teaspoon of paste per vanilla bean called for.

Yeast Fresh yeast is pretty much always my preference. It just works so much *better* than the dried packaged stuff, which can be unreliable. That said, I realize it's not always accessible. I have found it mostly at Italian and Polish grocery stores. The old-world crowd is obviously still demanding it, and I couldn't be happier. Most nice bakeries will also sell you some if you ask. It will keep in the refrigerator for a few weeks at least, so you can use its perishability as an excuse to make more delicious yeasted treats.

That said, because it can be hard to find, I have called for dried yeast in my recipes here. To substitute fresh use this formula:

1 teaspoon active dry yeast = 5.67 grams fresh yeast or 1 teaspoon instant yeast = 8.5 grams fresh yeast

I realize it's a little odd to begin with a jam recipe made from fruit that is in season for such a short time, but I hope you can track some down. Black raspberries are native to eastern North America, often found growing wild, but you can also plant them in your garden. The thing is, they are sublime, and so I can't help myself but open with this recipe. I'm not generally in the habit of encouraging the removal of seeds or pulp, but this is an exceedingly seedy fruit.

Black Raspberry Jam

Makes four 250 mL (8 oz) jars

1.44 kg (9 cups) black raspberries, divided

550 g (2¾ cups) sugar

45 mL (3 Tbsp) lemon juice

In a large bowl, combine 960 grams (6 cups) of the black raspberries with the sugar and lemon juice. Purée the remaining 480 grams (3 cups) of raspberries in a blender or food processor, then strain through a fine mesh sieve into a clean bowl, pushing to remove the seeds. Add the strained purée to the sugar mixture. Let it macerate, uncovered, for at least 15 minutes, or up to 1 week, in the refrigerator.

Prepare the jars (see page 20).

Transfer the mixture to a pot or preserving pan. Heat on medium-high and bring to a hard boil, stirring frequently. Be careful, as this jam has a tendency to really foam up and can even boil over if not watched closely. It won't be as obvious that it's done from the sheeting, so observe the way it thickens in the pan—you can feel it as you stir—and do a freezer plate test (see page 25).

When the setting point is reached, remove from the heat. Pour into the prepared jars to within ¼ to ⅛ inch of the rim. Remove any air bubbles, wipe the rims if necessary, seal, and invert for 1 to 2 minutes. Flip the jars right side up and let the jam sit, undisturbed, for 24 hours.

This cake is subtly sweet, is perfect for an afternoon treat, and keeps well for days. What more could you want? It works in a pinch for breakfast as well, would be most welcome at brunch, and wouldn't be amiss next to a glass of sherry in the evening. And whole grain on top of it all? I'm sold.

Coffee Cake

Makes one 10-inch tube cake

For the Streusel:

58 g (¼ cup) unsalted butter, melted, cooled

70 g (½ cup) whole spelt flour

67 g (⅓ cup) sugar

40 g (⅓ cup) ground hazelnuts

¼ tsp salt

For the Cake:

200 g (1 cup) sugar

115 g (½ cup) unsalted butter, melted, cooled

2 large eggs, at room temperature

2 tsp vanilla extract

175 g (1¼ cups) whole spelt flour

60 g (½ cup) ground hazelnuts

1½ tsp baking powder

½ tsp salt

180 g (¾ cup) sour cream

½ jar Black Raspberry Jam (page 52)

Icing sugar, for dusting (optional)

Preheat the oven to 350°F (175°C). Grease a 10-inch tube pan, preferably one with a removable bottom, with butter or nonstick spray and dust it with flour.

To make the streusel, in a small bowl combine the melted butter with the flour, sugar, ground hazelnuts, and salt. Rub everything together with your fingertips until the mixture is sandy and clumpy. Reserve in the refrigerator until ready to use, for up to 2 days, or in the freezer for up to 1 month.

To make the cake, in a large bowl, whisk together the sugar, melted butter, eggs, and vanilla. Switch to a spatula and gently fold in the flour, ground hazelnuts, baking powder, and salt. Fold in the sour cream until no white streaks remain.

Transfer the batter to the prepared pan. Top with the jam, leaving a ½-inch border on either side. Cover evenly with the streusel, pressing lightly so it adheres.

NOTES: *Sub in Raspberry Lambic Jam (page 91), Coffee, Date, & Pear Jam (page 198), or a good-quality store-bought blackberry or raspberry jam.*

Bake for 55 to 60 minutes, until a toothpick inserted into the center of the cake comes out with just a few moist crumbs attached or an instant read thermometer poked into the middle reads 210°F (99°C). Cool in the pan on a wire rack for 30 minutes before removing from the pan to cool completely. Dust with icing sugar before serving, if desired. Store at room temperature covered (such as under a cake dome) or wrapped in plastic for up to 5 days.

When I became the pastry chef for a bakery, I told them that I refused to make novelty scones full of crazy ingredients, and that candied ginger scones was as far as I would go. But when we started making oatmeal scones with currants and orange zest, my experimenting began to snowball. The key is to never make them too sweet—no glaze necessary. These cheesecake scones are nice for breakfast on the run, when you don't have time to lovingly slather a plain scone with drippy jam.

Cheesecake Scones

Makes 8 scones |

For the Cheesecake Chunks:

230 g (one 8 oz package) cream cheese, at room temperature

67 g (⅓ cup) sugar

1 large egg, at room temperature

½ tsp vanilla extract

60 g (¼ cup) sour cream

For the Scones:

420 g (3 cups) all-purpose flour

50 g (¼ cup) sugar, plus extra for sprinkling

2 Tbsp baking powder

¾ tsp salt

115 g (½ cup) unsalted butter, cold, cubed

250 mL (1 cup) heavy cream, plus extra for brushing

½ jar Black Raspberry Jam (page 52)

Make the cheesecake chunks the night before you plan to make the scones. Preheat the oven to 300°F (150°C). Grease a 5- x 9-inch loaf pan with butter and line with parchment paper.

In a bowl by hand (because it's a relatively small amount) or with a hand mixer or a stand mixer fitted with the paddle attachment, beat together the cream cheese and sugar until smooth and fluffy. Beat in the egg, followed by the vanilla extract. Fold in the sour cream until well blended, then pour into the pan, smoothing the top with a mini offset spatula.

Bake for 30 minutes, until just set. Let cool completely in the pan on a wire rack, then put it in the freezer, pan and all, to freeze overnight (cover if freezing longer than overnight).

Before making the scones, remove the cheesecake from the pan and cut it into roughly ½- to 1-inch chunks. Put them on a parchment-lined baking sheet and chill in the freezer until needed.

To make the scones, place the flour, sugar, baking powder, and salt in a stand mixer fitted with the paddle attachment. Mix on low speed for 30 seconds to combine. Add the butter and mix on medium-low until the butter is variously olive- to pea-sized pieces. You can stop the mixer and squish any large chunks between your thumb and forefinger to speed up the process. Toss in the cheesecake chunks and mix on low for a few seconds to disperse them. Then, with the mixer running on low, pour in the cream, followed by the jam, letting it go a few seconds more so that everything is raggedly combined.

Turn the dough out onto a floured surface and pat it into a 1-inch-thick shape (oval, square, whatever). Fold the dough in half and then give it a quarter turn, patting it back down to 1 inch thick. Repeat three times, ending by shaping it into a 9-inch-diameter circle (about 2 inches thick). Use a knife or bench scraper to cut the dough into eight equal triangles. You can bake them now if you must, but I prefer to freeze them overnight, as it gives a flakier result.

When you're ready to bake, preheat the oven to 375°F (190°C). Line a baking sheet with parchment paper. Arrange the scones 2 inches apart on the baking sheet. Brush the top with cream and sprinkle with sugar. Bake for 35 to 40 minutes, until golden and an instant read thermometer poked into one reads 210°F (99°C). Let cool at least slightly on the pan on a wire rack before serving.

Damsons are an English variety of plum whose main purpose in life is to become jam. Damson is one of my favorite jams in the entire world, and I would never alter it in any way. Are they kind of a pain in the butt to pit? Yes, okay, they are very small, which means a lot of pits. But you don't have to chop them, which makes up for it. I push the pits out with my thumb and leave it at that. The acidic, slightly astringent flesh melts into the jam, leaving big, toothsome pieces of peel. The flavor and texture are unparalleled.

If you substitute a different plum, which will be sweeter, you'll want to reduce the sugar by at least 10% (and probably chop them up).

 ## Damson Jam

Makes four 250 mL (8 oz) jars

1.22 kg (6½ cups) pitted damson plums (see note)

750 g (3¾ cups) sugar

60 mL (¼ cup) lemon juice

NOTE: *You'll need about 1.5 kg whole plums.*

In a large bowl, combine all of the ingredients and let macerate, uncovered, for at least 15 minutes, or up to 1 week, in the refrigerator.

Prepare the jars (see page 20).

Transfer the mixture to a pot or preserving pan. Heat on medium-high and bring to a hard boil, stirring frequently.

When the setting point is reached (see page 23), remove from the heat and pour into the prepared jars to within ¼ to ⅛ inch of the rim. Remove any air bubbles, wipe the rims if necessary, seal, and invert for 1 to 2 minutes. Flip the jars right side up and let the jam sit, undisturbed, for 24 hours.

Nigel Slater's genius marmalade ice cream inspired this recipe. He replaces most of the sugar required with marmalade, resulting in one of the most delicious and smoothest-textured homemade ice creams I've ever made. It is deeply rich with bitter orange flavor. I thought damsons would make an equally lovely ice cream—the jam is a bit higher in sugar and has a texture that sort of reminds me of marmalade thanks to the whole skin pieces. Consider adding some chopped toasted hazelnuts or walnuts, and enjoy after dinner with a glass of grappa. (You'll need an ice cream maker for this.)

Chocolate-Speckled Ice Cream

Serves 6 |

500 mL (2 cups) heavy cream

80 g (4) egg yolks

2 Tbsp sugar

380 g (1½ jars) Damson Jam (page 57)

115 g (4 oz) dark chocolate

NOTE: *Can sub Black Currant & Sweet Cherry Jam (page 96) or good-quality store-bought plum jam.*

In a heavy-bottomed pot over medium heat, begin to warm the cream. In the meantime, in a medium bowl, whisk the yolks with the sugar until pale and thick. When the cream comes to a boil, whisk it into the yolks in a slow, steady stream. Return the mixture to the pot and, over medium-low heat, stirring constantly, heat to 180°F (82°C), or until it thickens just enough to coat the back of a wooden spoon. Strain through a fine mesh sieve into a clean bowl, cover with plastic wrap, making sure it's touching the surface to prevent a skin from forming, and refrigerate overnight.

The next day, whisk the jam into the ice cream base and freeze according to your ice cream machine's instructions. About 10 minutes before it should be ready, in a heatproof bowl set over a pan of simmering water, or in the microwave in 20- to 30-second bursts, melt the chocolate. Set aside to cool slightly. When the ice cream is ready, with the machine running, slowly stream in the melted chocolate. Let the machine run

for about 1 minute to make sure the chocolate is well incorporated and the pieces get broken up.

Transfer to a reusable 1-liter (4-cup) container and cover the surface with wax paper before freezing for at least 3 hours before serving. The ice cream will keep for 2 weeks.

I absolutely love the ingenuity of bakers looking for ways to extend the life of their creations. By filling day-old croissants with rich almond cream (aka frangipane), bakers give the pastry a new life. The finished product depends a lot on the quality of croissant you buy, although this is also a situation where a subpar croissant might be vastly improved. As far as the jam goes, I always found damson was by far the very best foil for the richness of the pastry—unexpected, tart, textural, and richly flavored enough to be noticed. Prepare these the day before, up to the baking step. Just wrap and refrigerate them overnight, then pop them in the oven in the morning.

Almond Croissants

Makes 6 croissants |

6 (day-old) croissants

1 recipe Frangipane (page 233)

½ jar Damson Jam (page 57)

60 mL (¼ cup) whole milk

68 g (½ cup) sliced almonds

Icing sugar, for dusting

Preheat the oven to 350°F (175°C). Line a baking sheet with parchment paper.

Use a serrated knife to slice the croissants in half lengthwise, leaving just a little bit attached on the opposite side so you can open it up like a book. Using a mini offset spatula or butter knife, spread about 2½ tablespoons of frangipane over the base of each croissant, followed by 1 tablespoon of jam. Close the croissants and arrange them at least 1 inch apart on the prepared baking sheet.

Thin the remaining frangipane with milk, a little at a time, until it's a spreadable consistency (you may not need all of the milk). Spread the mixture onto the tops of the croissants. Shower with sliced almonds, pressing down so they adhere.

NOTE: *Can sub Cranberry &*
Clementine Jam (page 118), Summer
Pudding Jam (page 154), or a good-
quality store-bought plum jam.

Bake for 20 to 25 minutes, until golden brown. Let cool on the pan on a wire rack for about 15 minutes before dusting with some icing sugar. These are best eaten the day they are made.

Making jelly is one of the most satisfying tasks I know. There's just something about transforming juice into a solid that is so alchemical, the feeling amplified by the jewel-like transparency and hue. Turning whole fruit into juice may seem like a chore, but for the most part it's hands-off. That's right, you can spend the majority of the process watching TV or choreographing dance routines! It's mostly just simmering and dripping.

Consider saving the pulp to make fruit leather or to flavor kombucha. I've even painstakingly removed the cores of each spent half, dehydrated them, and added them to nougat with pecans and brown butter, which was superlative.

Crabapple Jelly

Makes four to five 250 mL (8 oz) jars

1.8 kg (16 cups) crabapples
1.25 L (5 cups) water
700 g (3½ cups) sugar
45 mL (3 Tbsp) lemon juice

Halve the crabapples (or quarter, if large), and remove the stems and blossom ends. Place them in a large pot with the water, and bring to a boil over high heat. Turn down the heat to medium-low and simmer, uncovered, until the crabapples are very soft and breaking down, about 30 minutes. Pour the mixture into a wet jelly bag (see page 15) suspended over a deep receptacle and let it drip overnight. It's very important never to squeeze the bag or force the pulp through—we want a juice mostly free from solids for a prize-winning crystalline jelly!

The next day, check that you have 1 liter (4 cups) of juice. If there's more, save the extra for lower-pectin jams (see page 198). If there's less, top it up with a little water.

Prepare your jars (see page 20).

Transfer the crabapple juice to a wide, heavy-bottomed pan and add the sugar and lemon juice. Bring to a boil over medium-high heat. Cook at a rolling boil, stirring frequently and skimming off any foam, until the setting point (see page 23) is reached. This jelly will fall off the spatula in big clumps.

Remove from the heat and pour into the hot jars to within ¼ to ⅛ inch of the rim. Wipe the rims if necessary, seal, and invert for 1 to 2 minutes. Flip right side up and let the jelly sit, undisturbed, for 24 hours.

My friend Carlin discovered the recipe that this one is inspired by in *Gourmet* 15 years ago, when barely anyone I knew had heard of brown butter. So called because they are shaped in the depression of a spoon, these cookies were a revelation, and I have made them every year since during the holiday season. Mine are a bit bigger than the original (they're so good you want them to be more than one bite), lightly spiced, and a little less crumbly. You must make them in advance, as they improve with age. They travel well too. I individually wrapped them like candies once and sent a pile to my friend Maggie (this book's illustrator) across the country for her birthday.

Spoon Cookies

Makes 18 to 20 sandwich cookies |

230 g (1 cup) Brown Butter (page 228)

280 g (2 cups) all-purpose flour

150 g (¾ cup) sugar

1 tsp baking soda

¼ tsp salt

¼ tsp Mixed Spice (page 233)

2 tsp vanilla extract

2–3 Tbsp Crabapple Jelly (page 63)

Melt the brown butter in a pot on the stovetop or in a microwave (it only needs about 45 seconds—keep an eye on it so it doesn't burn), then transfer to a medium bowl and stir in the flour, sugar, baking soda, salt, mixed spice, and vanilla. The dough will be very soft. Wrap it in plastic wrap and let it sit for 1 to 2 hours at room temperature so that it's easier to handle (you can also refrigerate it for a few days, but note that it will take a few hours to temper once pulled from the refrigerator before you can shape it).

Preheat the oven to 325°F (160°C). Line a baking sheet with parchment paper.

Using a spoon with a nice shape (I use a round soup spoon with a 1-tablespoon capacity), push in the dough flush with the spoon then slide it out onto the baking sheet. Repeat until all the dough is shaped, placing the pieces 1 inch apart. You're aiming for 36 to 40 evenly sized pieces.

Bake until deep golden brown, about 15 minutes. Let cool completely on the pan on a wire rack.

Spread a thin layer of jelly onto the bottom of one cookie and sandwich it with another. Repeat with the remaining cookies and jelly.

Store the sandwich cookies, stacked between sheets of wax paper, in an airtight container at room temperature for at least 2 days before eating and up to 2 weeks. I know it's a long time, but they will taste so much better!

A sablé Breton is a classic French cookie from Brittany, known for its butter and buckwheat. I first learned to make the golden, all-purpose flour version from chef Patrice Demers in Montreal, where we made tiny ones to serve as mignardises and larger, cakier ones for plated desserts. Once I discovered the buckwheat flour version, however, I was hooked.

I had toyed with this particular recipe idea for years. They have the visual appeal of a cupcake but are full of surprising, contrasting textures and flavors—the crumbly, earthy buckwheat base, vibrant and acidic crabapple jelly hiding within, and toasty meringue topping made with fragrant honey instead of sugar.

Breton Buckwheat Tarts

Makes 12 tarts |

For the Buckwheat Sablés:

175 g (1¼ cups) all-purpose flour

105 g (¾ cup + 2 Tbsp) buckwheat flour

1 Tbsp baking powder

¾ tsp salt

100 g (5) egg yolks

300 g (1½ cups) sugar

187 g (¾ cup + 1 Tbsp) unsalted butter, softened

To Finish:

½ jar Crabapple Jelly (page 63)

180 g (½ cup + ½ Tbsp) honey

90 g (3) egg whites

To make the buckwheat sablés, in a small bowl, combine the flours, baking powder, and salt. Set aside.

In a stand mixer fitted with the whisk attachment, whip the yolks and sugar on high speed until the ribbon stage, when the mixture is pale and thick and leaves ribbon-like trails that take a moment to sink back in when the whisk is lifted. Switch to the paddle attachment and add the dry ingredients, mixing on low just to combine. Add the butter and mix until homogeneous.

Roll the dough between two pieces of parchment paper to ½ inch thick. Transfer carefully to the refrigerator and chill until firm, at least 1 hour and up to overnight.

Once it's chilled, preheat the oven to 325°F (160°C) and generously grease a 12-cup muffin tin with butter.

Peel the parchment paper off each side of the dough. Cut out one dozen 2½-inch rounds (you can gather the scraps and roll again to make a thinner version, or crumble and use in place of graham cracker crumbs to make a great cheesecake base).

Bake for 20 minutes, or until the sablés are golden and firm around the edges. Let cool completely in the pan on a wire rack.

To finish, unmold the sablés and fill each with about 2 teaspoons of jelly.

To make the meringue, in the bowl of a stand mixer set over a pot of simmering water (making sure the bowl doesn't touch the water), whisk together (by hand) the honey and egg whites. Heat, whisking constantly, until the mixture is warm to the touch. Transfer the bowl to the stand mixer, fitted with the whisk attachment, and whip on high speed until stiff, glossy, and just warm.

Using a piping bag fitted with a no. 6 plain tip, or using a spoon (though it won't look as decorative), top the sablés with a generous crown of meringue, covering the jelly completely. Using a blowtorch, or placing them briefly under the broiler, brown the meringue.

These are best eaten the day they're made but will keep in an airtight container at room temperature overnight—they'll just be less texturally contrasting, as the jelly soaks into the sablé and softens it.

Sliced fruit Seville marmalade is more jelly than peel, gorgeously refracting light. While cooking, it flakes off the spatula, pectin-rich, in textbook style. It uses Seville oranges—high in pectin, rich in flavor, and sour as lemons, which all helps balance the sugar—a classic for marmalade. Look for them from January to early March. They are incomparable.

A Different Seville Marmalade

Makes seven 250 mL (8 oz) jars

700 g (about 4) Seville oranges
1.7 liters (6¾ cups) water
1.4 kg (7 cups) sugar
45 mL (3 Tbsp) lemon juice

Rinse the oranges and cut them in half. Juice the oranges, reserving the seeds and peels, and transfer the juice to a large pot and add water. Pull the membranes from the juiced orange halves and reserve with the seeds. Slice the peels ⅛ inch thick and add to the pot. Coarsely chop the reserved seeds and membranes, place them in a mesh bag, and add to the pot. Cover and soak overnight for at least 12 hours but no more than 16.

The next day, bring the mixture (mesh bag included) to a boil over high heat. Turn down the heat to medium and simmer, uncovered, until the oranges are very soft and the mixture has reduced by about two-thirds, about 1 hour. Remove the mesh bag, and using a spatula, press down to extract all of the juice.

Prepare the jars (see page 20).

Add the sugar and lemon juice to the pot. Heat on medium-high and bring to a hard boil, stirring frequently. When the setting point is reached (see page 23), remove from the heat and pour into the prepared jars to within ¼ to ⅛ inch of the rim. Remove any air bubbles, wipe the rims, seal, and invert for 1 to 2 minutes. Flip right side up and let the marmalade sit, undisturbed, for 24 hours.

Natasha Pickowicz is a very talented pastry chef based in NYC, as well as an activist specializing in radical bake sales. She is also the person who got me started teaching preserving classes (thanks, Natasha!). I asked her to create a new twist on the classic dish crepes Suzette, and she came up with this gorgeous showstopper. As she puts it, "These lacy, nutty crepes are draped over a hidden core of milky ice cream and Camilla's bright and deliciously bitter Seville orange marmalade. The crepes are sprinkled with sugar and brûléed with a torch to get them crisp and caramelized, but it works melted out under a regular home oven broiler, too!"

Brûléed Buckwheat Crepes

Makes twelve 6-inch crepes |

For the Crepes:

60 g (½ cup) buckwheat flour

60 g (¼ cup + 3 Tbsp) all-purpose flour

1 Tbsp sugar

¾ tsp salt

2 large eggs

350 mL (1⅓ cups + 1 Tbsp) skim milk

1 Tbsp melted unsalted butter, cooled

1 tsp vanilla extract

To Assemble:

Sugar, for sprinkling

1 pint fior di latte gelato or sweet cream ice cream

1 jar A Different Seville Marmalade (page 70)

Flaky salt

Preheat the oven to 300°F (150°C).

Spread out both flours in a skillet or on a sheet tray and lightly toast in the oven until fragrant, about 10 to 15 minutes. Set aside to cool. (You can do this in advance. Natasha loves to keep jars of toasted flours on hand for cookie and cake baking, too.)

To cook the crepes, in a blender, combine the cooled toasted flours with the sugar, salt, eggs, milk, melted butter, and vanilla. Blend until smooth. Set aside and chill in the refrigerator for at least 1 hour before baking.

To make the crepes, preheat a 6- to 8-inch nonstick skillet over medium heat and very lightly coat with nonstick cooking spray. Stir the chilled crepe batter when you take it out of the refrigerator. It should run off a spoon in a smooth and runny stream when lifted. If it looks too thick, stir in some room-temperature water a spoonful at a time to loosen it up.

NOTE: *Can sub Crabapple Jelly (page 63), Damson Jam (page 57), or a good-quality store-bought Seville orange marmalade.*

Using a large spoon or ice cream scoop, pour just enough batter into the skillet to barely cover the surface of the pan, tilting the skillet to evenly coat it. Cook for 1 minute, or until the crepe looks set, then gently flip (a mini offset spatula can be helpful here) and cook for 1 more minute. Remove from the pan and set aside on a clean plate. Repeat until all the crepes are done, adding a layer of nonstick cooking spray to the skillet between each.

To assemble, place one crepe at a time on a piece of aluminum foil. Sprinkle one side of the crepe evenly with sugar to coat. Using a blowtorch, brûlée until the sugar is melted and caramelized, or place under a broiler until golden and bubbling.

While the sugar is still sticky and not "set," scrunch the foil to gently ruffle up the crepe, creating a tent shape and big folds and nice movement. As the sugar sets, the crepe will form a voluminous bucket shape. Repeat.

To plate, scoop the gelato onto the center of a plate or wide, shallow bowl. Gently press down on the scoop to create a wide depression. Fill this with a generous spoonful of marmalade. Sprinkle with a nice flaky salt of your choosing. Gently place the brûléed crepe "cage" on top. Eat immediately! It's so delicious when the crepe is still warm from the torch and the ice cream gets a little melty.

I met Michelle Marek—pastry chef, chef, preserving enthusiast, inveterate crafter, and Vermont lover—before either of us ever went to pastry school, but she's always been one of the best cooks I've ever known, armed with a natural skill and confidence I envy. We've been lucky enough to work together at a few spots over the years, and I always work better and am more inspired when we're together. She developed one of the best, and easiest, mini baba au rhum recipes I've ever encountered for a magazine, so I begged her to create a full-sized marmalade version for this book. True to form, she outdid herself.

Whisky Baba

Serves 10 to 12 | 🥄🥄🥄

For the Baba:

60 mL (¼ cup) half and half cream

1½ tsp instant yeast

2 Tbsp A Different Seville Marmalade (page 70), chopped

2 Tbsp warm water

1 large egg, room temperature

20 g (1) egg yolk

140 g (1 cup) all-purpose flour

1½ tsp sugar

½ tsp salt

58 g (¼ cup) butter, softened, cubed

1 tsp grated orange zest

Heat the cream in a small saucepan to just warm, 100°F to 110°F (38°C to 43°C).

In a stand mixer fitted with the paddle attachment, place the cream and yeast. Let stand for 5 minutes, until the yeast has dissolved. On low speed, mix in the chopped marmalade and water, followed by the egg and yolk. Add the flour, sugar, and salt and mix until smooth. Add the butter a bit at a time, mixing well between additions. Add the zest and mix until well distributed. Cover the bowl with plastic wrap and let the dough rise at room temperature until doubled. This will take about 45 minutes.

Generously grease a 10-cup Bundt pan with butter.

Gently scrape the dough from the sides of the bowl, and grab it in one piece with your hands. Working quickly and with courage, insert your thumbs into the

For the Syrup:

200 g (1 cup) sugar

⅓ jar A Different Seville Marmalade (page 70)

125 mL (½ cup) water

125 mL (½ cup) whisk(e)y (a mild one like Glenlivet or Bushmills)

To Serve:

250 mL (1 cup) heavy cream

2 Tbsp sugar

NOTE: *Can sub a good-quality store-bought Seville orange marmalade.*

---

center of the dough and pull it into a donut shape. Place the dough in the Bundt pan. Cover with plastic wrap and let the dough rise at room temperature until doubled. This rise will take about 20 minutes.

Meanwhile, preheat the oven to 350°F (175°C).

Remove the plastic wrap and bake for about 25 minutes, until golden brown and an instant read thermometer inserted into the middle reads 210°F (99°C).

Let cool in the pan on a wire rack for 5 minutes, then unmold and let cool for 15 minutes more. (It won't be completely cool, but that's okay. You want it warmish.)

While it cools, make the syrup. Combine the sugar, marmalade, and water in a small pot and bring to a boil over medium heat. Once the sugar has dissolved, remove the pot from the heat and add the whisky. Stir to combine. If there are large pieces of peel in the syrup, set them aside for serving.

Place the warm baba on the cooling rack and place the rack over a large bowl. Slowly and carefully begin to ladle the hot syrup from the bowl over the baba. Do this a few times, evenly distributing it, until only 125 mL (½ cup) remains. Let cool completely. Reserve the remaining syrup.

Just before serving, in a stand mixer fitted with the whisk attachment, whip the cream and sugar together on high speed until soft peaks form. Serve the baba with a drizzle of the reserved syrup, a dollop of whipped cream, and a few pieces of candied peel. This is best the day it is made, but any leftovers can be stored, covered, in the refrigerator for up to 3 days.

A word of warning—rhubarb jam is high maintenance. Toward the end of the cooking time, you will have to stir it almost constantly because otherwise it will stick. And when you stir, be prepared for it to spit violently, which means this is not the time to wear a silk shirt or a cashmere sweater (two things I am known to cavalierly wear while making jam). However, this version is absolutely worth all of the trouble. Made with Amarena cherries, candied Italian cherries often used to garnish cocktails, it will reward you with one of the prettiest, most delicious jams you've ever met.

Rhubarb & Amarena Cherry Jam

Makes six 250 mL (8 oz) jars

1.2 kg (8 cups) chopped rhubarb

725 g (3½ cups + 2 Tbsp) sugar

60 mL (¼ cup) lemon juice

130 g (½ cup) Amarena cherries

2 Tbsp maraschino liqueur (optional) (see note)

NOTE: *If you buy a bottle of maraschino liqueur especially for this recipe, you can make an Aviation cocktail (one of my favorites, just look online) to enjoy and take the edge off while you cook.*

In a large bowl, combine the rhubarb, sugar, and lemon juice and macerate for at least 15 minutes, or up to 1 week, covered, in the refrigerator.

Coarsely chop the cherries and throw them into the macerated mix.

Prepare the jars (see page 20).

Transfer the mixture to a pot or preserving pan. Heat on medium-high and bring to a hard boil, stirring constantly to prevent it from sticking. Because this spits prodigiously, use your longest spatula and wear an old long-sleeved top!

When the setting point is reached (see page 23), remove from the heat and add the liqueur, if using. Pour into the prepared jars to within ¼ to ⅛ inch of the rim. Remove any air bubbles, wipe the rims if necessary, seal, and invert for 1 to 2 minutes. Flip right side up and let the jam sit, undisturbed, for 24 hours.

My father is an excellent cook but has an unsavory penchant for giving perfectly reasonable foods horrible names—mucko for leftover mashed potatoes mixed with gravy and shredded meat, scum for coffee's crema. This makes sense, though, as he hails from England, a country whose medieval cookbooks contain recipes for a stew called Garbage. Then, of course, there's Eton Mess, which is traditionally made of whipped cream mixed with crushed meringues and fresh strawberries. It's a little on the nose (it does look a bit of a mess), but it lands more squarely in the realm of charmingly funny than totally off-putting. Because I cannot easily think of rhubarb without custard, I've added some to the cream and forgone the strawberries in favor of cherries to darkly stain it and make it look even messier.

Eton Mess

Serves 6 | ♩♩

For the Meringues:

60 g (2) egg whites, room temperature

120 g (½ cup + 2 Tbsp) sugar

1½ Tbsp custard powder (optional) (such as Bird's)

To make the meringues, preheat the oven to 250°F (121°C). Line a half sheet pan with parchment paper.

In a stand mixer fitted with the whisk attachment, whisk the egg whites on medium-high speed until soft peaks form. With the machine running, gradually add the sugar and continue to whip until the mixture holds firm peaks. Fold in the custard powder, if using. Transfer the mixture to a piping bag fitted with a large plain tip and pipe long tubes or ropes of meringue— to give it a futuristic look—onto the prepared baking sheet. You can also spread it out thinly using an offset spatula or pipe little kisses (in which case, use a large open star tip)—up to you!

For the Cream:

125 mL (½ cup) whole milk

50 g (4 Tbsp) sugar, divided

140 g (7) egg yolks

500 mL (2 cups) heavy cream, cold

1–2 Tbsp maraschino liqueur (optional)

To Finish:

½ jar Rhubarb & Amarena Cherry Jam
(page 78)

300 g (2 cups) pitted fresh or thawed
frozen black cherries

———————

NOTE: *Can sub Rhubarb Lemonade
Jam with Elderflower (page 159)
(sub strawberries for cherries),
Black Currant & Sweet Cherry
Jam (page 96), or a good-quality
store-bought rhubarb or cherry jam
(or a mix of the two!).*

———————

Bake for 45 minutes, until firm and dry. If possible,
turn off the oven and let the meringue cool inside with
the door ajar, or just cool on the pan on a wire rack.

Once cool, you can store them in an airtight container.
They'll keep for ages if stored in a cool, dry place.

To make the cream, combine the milk with 2 tablespoons of the sugar in a small pot and bring to a
simmer over medium heat. In the meantime, whisk
the yolks with the remaining sugar in a medium bowl
until they are well combined and a few shades paler.
Temper the eggs by slowly streaming the hot milk
into the yolk mixture, whisking constantly, and
then transfer the mixture back to the pot. Cook
on medium-low heat, stirring constantly, until the
mixture reaches 180°F (82°C) or coats the back of
a wooden spoon. Immediately remove from the heat
and strain through a fine mesh sieve into a heatproof
bowl. Cover with plastic wrap, making sure it's
touching the surface so a skin doesn't form, and
refrigerate for at least a few hours, or up to 2 days.

To finish, in a stand mixer fitted with the whisk
attachment, whip the chilled custard with the heavy
cream and liqueur, if using, on medium-high speed
until firm peaks form. Break up the meringue into
bite-sized pieces and fold into the cream along with
the jam and cherries. Portion and serve. Store any
leftovers in the freezer in an airtight container with
a sheet of wax paper directly on the surface. It makes
for a delicious frozen treat for another day.

Great for a picnic or birthday party, this looks like a giant Pop-Tart straight out of a kid's Candyland dream world, and I love it. I was originally going to make hand pies with this filling, but the large version had such a big impact, especially with that one cherry right in the middle, that I had to change tack. Using the syrup from the Amarena cherries for the glaze gives it a lovely cherry flavor and a beautiful natural pink color.

Rhubarb, Cherry, & Custard Slab Pie

Makes 1 large slab pie, 10 to 12 servings |

For the Galette:

2 recipes Galette Dough (single crust) (page 232)

1 recipe Pastry Cream (page 229)

1 jar Rhubarb & Amarena Cherry Jam (page 78)

For the Glaze:

250 g (2 cups) icing sugar

30–60 mL (2–4 Tbsp) syrup from a jar of Amarena cherries

30–60 mL (2–4 Tbsp) heavy cream

1 Amarena cherry, preferably with stem

To make the galette, preheat the oven to 375°F (190°C). Line a baking sheet with parchment paper.

On a lightly floured surface, roll out one disk of the galette dough into a rectangle approximately 12 x 15 inches and slide it onto the baking sheet.

Give the pastry cream a few judicious stirs to smooth it, then, using an offset spatula, spread it evenly over the rectangle, leaving a 1-inch border all around. Repeat with the jam. Brush the border with cold water.

Roll the second disk of galette dough to the same dimensions. Carefully lift it and place it over the first, pressing around the edges to adhere. Using kitchen scissors or a paring knife, trim any jagged edges. Use two fingers of one hand to hold the dough and the thumb of the other to push, crimp the edges as you would a pie. Cut three or four slits in the top to let the steam escape.

Refrigerate the galette for about 30 minutes, or up to overnight, until firm. (It can also be frozen, well wrapped, for up to 1 month. Bake from frozen; it may take a little longer to bake.)

Bake for about 45 minutes, until the top is golden brown and the jam is bubbling through the vents in the pastry. Let cool completely on a wire rack.

To make the glaze, in a medium bowl, whisk the icing sugar with 2 tablespoons each of the syrup and cream until it has a pouring consistency, adding more if necessary. Pour it onto the pastry, spreading it evenly with a mini offset spatula and leaving a border of crimped edge all around. Place the single cherry in the center. Let the glaze set at room temperature for at least 30 minutes before serving.

The slab pie is best the day it is made, but any leftovers can be stored in an airtight container at room temperature for up to 2 days.

Recipe pictured on the title page

Despite strawberry jam being one of the more difficult jams to master, it's often the first thing novice preservers try their hand at. Strawberries have very low pectin levels and tend to foam formidably. That said, it's easy enough to get a nice soft set with practice. In this recipe, the sweet strawberries get a welcome dose of acidity from the passion fruit (although it is dampened by cooking, which is why we add the citric acid at the end), as well as the great textural crunch of the seeds. The passion fruit also makes for a polka-dot jam, which is undeniably cool.

 # Strawberry & Passion Fruit Jam

Makes five 250 mL (8 oz) jars

1.2 kg (8 cups) rinsed, hulled strawberries

600 g (3 cups) sugar

160 g (⅔ cup) passion fruit pulp, from about 6 passion fruit

60 mL (¼ cup) lemon juice

½ tsp citric acid

In a large bowl, combine the strawberries, sugar, pulp, and lemon juice and let macerate for at least 15 minutes, or up to 1 week, covered, in the refrigerator.

Prepare the jars (see page 20).

Once the sugar has drawn out some juice and softened up the strawberries, mash them by hand and squeeze them with your fists. Not only is this fun, it also makes for a rough, uneven texture that I love. It also takes 5% of the time it would take to chop them all up with a knife. If this method freaks you out, wear latex gloves!

Transfer the mixture to a pot or preserving pan over medium-high heat. Bring to a hard boil, stirring frequently.

When the setting point is reached (see page 23), remove from the heat and add the citric acid, stirring well to combine. Pour into the prepared jars to within ¼ to ⅛ inch of the rim. Remove any air bubbles, wipe the rims if necessary, seal, and invert for 1 to 2 minutes. Flip right side up and let the jam sit, undisturbed, for 24 hours.

When I was growing up, my favorite birthday cake was confetti angel food cake made from the boxed mix, particularly the crusty top (or bottom, once unmolded), which I would sneakily tear chunks off. I didn't make angel food cake from scratch until I was in my early 20s, but I immediately fell in love with the textural experience of making it. One cookbook I had suggested mixing it by hand (as in, with your whole bare arm as it's a voluminous mix), and it's such a tactile treat, the feeling of airy egg whites mixing with fine cake flour. Make this for that reason, but also to delight children and adults alike. The jam brings a little acidity that takes it out of the realm of the ordinary angel food cake.

Angel Food Cake

Makes one 10-inch tube cake |

For the Cake:

130 g (1 cup + 1 Tbsp + 1 tsp) cake flour

300 g (1½ cups) sugar, divided

330 g (11) egg whites, at room temperature

2 Tbsp lemon juice

1 tsp vanilla extract

¼ tsp salt

½ jar Strawberry & Passion Fruit Jam (page 84)

To make the cake, preheat the oven to 350°F (175°C). DO NOT grease the tube pan for this cake, or prepare it in any other way. In fact, it's even better if your pan isn't nonstick, as this cake wants to be able to hold onto the sides of the pan to climb up.

Sift the cake flour with 100 grams (½ cup) of the sugar.

In a stand mixer fitted with the whisk attachment, whip the egg whites on medium speed until white and foamy. With the machine running, add the lemon juice, vanilla, and salt. Increase the speed to medium-high, beat until soft peaks form, and then gradually add the remaining 200 grams (1 cup) of sugar. Continue to beat until firm peaks form and the tip of the peak just falls over—we don't want stiff peaks, because they'll make it hard to fold in the flour. Remove the whisk and the bowl from the mixer.

To Finish:

Icing sugar, for dusting

OR

250 ml (1 cup) heavy cream

2 Tbsp icing sugar

Flesh and seeds from 1 passion fruit

2–3 fresh strawberries, sliced

NOTE: *Can sub Summer Pudding Jam (page 154) (decorate with summer berries), Black Raspberry Jam (page 52) (decorate with multicolored raspberries), or good-quality store-bought strawberry jam.*

Sprinkle one-third of the sifted flour and sugar mixture over the whites and, using a clean hand, gently fold it in—I know, using a bare hand may seem freaky, but it's the best way to find any hidden pockets of unmixed flour. You could also use a spatula or balloon whisk if the thought of using your hand is really too much. Repeat twice, for a total of three mixes. Using a spatula, gently fold in the jam. Do not overmix. You want streaks throughout.

Transfer the batter to the pan, smoothing out the top with a small offset spatula or butter knife. Run a butter knife through the batter to remove any large air bubbles.

Bake for 40 to 45 minutes, or until golden and firm and an instant read thermometer inserted in the center of the cake reads 208°F (97°C). Immediately invert the pan and let the cake cool completely. If your pan has little legs for inversion, that's perfect. Otherwise, put the hole over the neck of a wine bottle.

Once the cake has cooled, use a metal spatula to loosen it from the pan before unmolding onto a serving platter.

You could serve it just like that, dusted with a little icing sugar. Or, for a special touch, in a stand mixer fitted with the whisk attachment, whip the cream with the icing sugar on high speed until stiff peaks form. Pile on top of the cake and decorate with the passion fruit and strawberries.

If you're not serving immediately, refrigerate until needed (if it's garnished with cream). This is best the day it is made, but it will keep, covered (in the refrigerator, if it's garnished with cream), for up to 3 days.

When I found a recipe for fluffy yeasted angel biscuits in one of my grandmother's recipe folders that I in no way recall her making, I knew I had to try them. I had heard somewhere you can deep-fry them to make donuts, so I went straight there, since a pot of boiling oil is usually where my deepest affections lie. If you don't have time to make the jam filling, they are nearly as incredible simply rolled in icing sugar. You could also cut out the center of the round to make the traditional donut shape and glaze them with a mixture of jam and icing sugar instead of filling them. This is the easiest version of yeasted dough I have ever encountered, and the result is as tender as a cake donut. The recipe doubles easily if you're having a donut party. What I am saying is that this is a win-win.

Angel Biscuit Donuts

Makes 10 donuts |

For the Donuts:

60 mL (¼ cup) water

1⅛ tsp (½ envelope) active dry yeast

350 g (2½ cups) all-purpose flour

2 Tbsp sugar

½ tsp baking powder

½ tsp baking soda

½ tsp salt

2 Tbsp unsalted butter, cold, cubed

2 Tbsp lard or shortening, cold, cubed

250 mL (1 cup) buttermilk

2 L (8 cups) neutral oil, for frying

To make the donuts, heat the water in a small saucepan to just warm, 100°F to 110°F (38°C to 43°C). Whisk in the yeast and let stand for 5 minutes, until foamy.

In a stand mixer fitted with the paddle attachment, mix together the flour, sugar, baking powder, baking soda, and salt on low speed. Increase the speed to medium-low, and mix in the butter and lard until the mixture resembles coarse crumbs. Remove the bowl from the stand mixer, add the yeast mixture and buttermilk, and stir with a wooden spoon to combine. Cover and refrigerate for 1 hour.

In a large, heavy-bottomed pot, heat the oil to 360°F (182°C). Set a wire rack over a rimmed baking sheet.

To Finish:

½ jar Strawberry & Passion Fruit Jam
   (page 84)

7 g (¼ cup) freeze-dried strawberries

63 g (½ cup) icing sugar

———————

NOTE: *Can sub Summer Pudding
Jam (page 154) or a good-quality
store-bought strawberry jam.*

———————

On a floured surface, knead the dough five times.
Using a rolling pin, roll the dough until it's ½ inch
thick. Cut out 10 rounds with a 2¾-inch plain cutter.

Being careful not to crowd the pan, fry the donuts,
four or five at a time, for 1 to 2 minutes per side, until
golden brown. Use a pair of chopsticks (I find they are
the easiest) to turn them and transfer them to the wire
rack. Let cool completely.

To finish, fill a pastry bag fitted with a small French
tip with the jam. Use a spice grinder to grind the
freeze-dried strawberries. Transfer the strawberries
to a medium bowl, add the icing sugar, and whisk
them together.

Once the donuts are cool enough to touch (it won't
take long), fill them with 1 teaspoon or so of the
jam, piercing the flattest side with the pointy tip,
then roll them in the icing sugar mixture so they
are well coated.

Eat as soon as possible! Like all donuts, these are best
the day they are made and don't keep particularly well.

Boiling a bottle of raspberry beer down into a concentrate and adding it to raspberry jam gets you raspberry jam squared. The raspberries taste more *raspberry* somehow than you ever thought possible, and the maltiness of the beer is an extra little indefinable taste that makes you want to eat the whole jar. Maybe she's born with it; maybe it's beer.

I never mash my raspberries. Instead, I let the heat break them down in the hopes that in the end some will still be nearly whole, floating in a glossy, seedy sea.

 # Raspberry Lambic Jam

Makes four 250 mL (8 oz) jars

1 (750 mL) bottle raspberry lambic beer (such as Lindemans)

1.2 kg (9½ cups) raspberries

600 g (3 cups) sugar

60 mL (¼ cup) lemon juice

Pour the beer into a large pot and bring to a boil over high heat. Boil until it reduces by two-thirds, about 30 minutes. You want about 250 mL (1 cup) of concentrated liquid.

While the beer is reducing, combine the raspberries, sugar, and lemon juice in a bowl and let macerate for at least 15 minutes, or up to 1 week, covered, in the refrigerator.

Prepare the jars (see page 20).

Transfer the macerated fruit to a pot or preserving pan and add the reduced beer. Heat on medium-high and bring to a hard boil, stirring frequently.

When the setting point is reached (see page 23), remove from the heat and pour into the prepared jars to within ¼ to ⅛ inch of the rim. Wipe the rims if necessary, seal, and invert for 1 to 2 minutes. Flip right side up and let the jam sit, undisturbed, for 24 hours.

I'm old-fashioned. Yes, I have plenty of recipes bookmarked online, but I also have binders full of recipes, just like my grandmothers did. It's a good thing, too—for some mysterious reason my trusty ginger cookie recipe suddenly stopped working. Fortunately, I found a childishly handwritten recipe titled "Amy's Ginger Crinkles," which, after a few modifications, worked perfectly. Who was Amy? I don't remember, but I suppose she was someone whose cookies I admired when I was younger. So, thank you, Amy. Now everyone gets to find out how astonishingly good a ginger and rye cookie is when sandwiched with raspberry jam. I'm tempted to call it a revelation, but I'll let you decide.

Rye & Ginger Sandwich Cookies

Makes 18 sandwich cookies |

140 g (1 cup) all-purpose flour

140 g (1 cup) whole rye flour

2½ tsp ground ginger

2 tsp baking soda

½ tsp ground cinnamon

½ tsp ground cloves

½ tsp salt

200 g (1 cup) sugar, plus more
for coating

165 mL (⅔ cup) neutral oil

80 g (¼ cup) molasses

1 egg

½ jar Raspberry Lambic Jam
(page 91)

Preheat the oven to 350°F (175°C). Line two baking sheets with parchment paper.

In a medium bowl, combine the flours, ginger, baking soda, cinnamon, cloves, and salt. Set aside.

In a large bowl, combine the sugar, oil, molasses, and egg, beating until homogeneous and emulsified. Add the dry ingredients and mix to combine.

In a shallow bowl, pour some sugar for coating. Use a ½-ounce ice cream scoop to form 36 balls of dough (about 1 tablespoon each) and roll each in the sugar to coat. Transfer to the baking sheets, placed at least 2 inches apart, and flatten slightly with your palm. Bake for about 10 minutes, until the cookies are cracked and golden around the edges. Let cool completely on the pan on a wire rack.

NOTE: *Can sub Crabapple Jelly (page 63), Damson Jam (page 57), or good-quality store-bought raspberry jam.*

Take two similarly shaped and sized cookies, use an offset spatula to spread about 1 teaspoon of jam onto the flat side of one cookie, and then press gently to sandwich it with the matching cookie.

These will keep in an airtight container at room temperature for up to 3 days.

Not unlike an English fool, cranachan is a Scottish dessert very similar to the cocktail Atholl Brose, named after the Earl of Atholl who apparently captured a rebel in 1475 by spiking his well with whisky, honey, and oats. This caused the man to be either so delighted or so intoxicated that he was easily subdued. I first found this in a breakfast cookbook (turns out cranachan is also very similar to the Scottish breakfast called crowdie), so I've subbed yogurt in for part of the cream, which brings a little acidity and some probiotics.

Cranachan

Serves 5 to 6

92 g (½ cup) steel cut oats

⅓ jar Raspberry Lambic Jam (page 91)

250 g (1½ cups) raspberries

375 mL (1½ cups) heavy cream

125 g (½ cup) thick yogurt

2 Tbsp honey, plus more for drizzling

2 Tbsp whisky

NOTE: *Can sub good-quality store-bought raspberry jam.*

In a dry skillet over medium-high heat, toast the oats, stirring often until they are golden and smell toasty. This should only take a few minutes. Transfer them to a bowl. Reserve about 1½ tablespoons for sprinkling over the finished dessert.

In a small pot over medium heat, or in the microwave (for 30 seconds to 1 minute), melt the jam and fold it into the fresh raspberries, mashing them a bit with the back of a spoon.

In a stand mixer fitted with the whisk attachment, whip the cream with the yogurt, honey, and whisky on high speed until stiff peaks form. Fold in the toasted oats and the raspberry mixture, then divide it between five or six 6-ounce ramekins, teacups, or 250 mL (8-ounce) jars. Refrigerate, uncovered, for 1 to 2 hours to set. Before serving, drizzle each serving with honey and sprinkle with the reserved toasted oats.

Cranachan is best served the day it is made, but any leftovers can be kept in the refrigerator, covered, for up to 2 days.

For a long time I considered black currant jam to be the pinnacle of jam and would never have considered cutting it with any "inferior" fruits. Then one day I just didn't have enough black currants, so I dialed back the sugar and threw in some black cherries, thinking the colors at least matched. The result was different—but at least as good as plain black currant jam. The cherries offer a meaty textural contrast to the seedy currants and cut the musky acidity with a little red fruit romanticism.

Black Currant & Sweet Cherry Jam

Makes five 250 mL (8 oz) jars

600 g (4 cups) topped and tailed black currants

575 g (4 cups) halved, pitted sweet cherries

675 g (3¼ cups + 2 Tbsp) sugar

75 mL (5 Tbsp) lemon juice

In a large bowl, combine all of the ingredients and let macerate for at least 15 minutes, or up to 1 week, covered, in the refrigerator.

Prepare the jars (see page 20).

Transfer the mixture to a pot or preserving pan. Heat on medium-high and bring to a hard boil, stirring frequently.

When the setting point is reached (see page 23), remove from the heat and ladle into the prepared jars to within ¼ to ⅛ inch of the rim. Remove any air bubbles, wipe the rims if necessary, seal, and invert for 1 to 2 minutes. Flip right side up and let the jam sit, undisturbed, for 24 hours.

Linzertorte, a sort of rich and nutty jam pie hailing from Austria, is apparently one of the oldest cakes in the world. I have no idea about the veracity of that statement, but it's easy to see why this has stayed in the world's dessert repertoire for so long. It's absolutely delicious. It's traditionally made with raspberry jam, and in this version the black currant and cherry flavors lend a similar acidity but more texture. And I added chocolate just because . . . it's chocolate.

Chocolate Linzertorte

Makes one 9-inch tart |

100 g (3½ oz) dark chocolate

230 g (1 cup) unsalted butter, softened

200 g (1 cup) sugar

40 g (2) egg yolks

1 tsp vanilla extract

280 g (2 cups) all-purpose flour

90 g (¾ cup) ground almonds

60 g (½ cup) ground hazelnuts

26 g (¼ cup) cocoa powder

½ tsp baking powder

½ tsp salt

2 jars Black Currant & Sweet Cherry
   Jam (page 96)

Unsweetened whipped cream,
   for serving

Grease a deep 9-inch tart pan (with a removable bottom) or springform pan with butter or nonstick spray.

In a heatproof bowl set over a pot of simmering water, or in the microwave in 20- to 30-second bursts, melt the chocolate. Set aside to cool slightly.

In a stand mixer fitted with the paddle attachment, cream the butter and sugar on medium speed until well combined. Beat in the egg yolks one by one, followed by the melted chocolate and vanilla. Scrape down the sides of the bowl.

Add the flour, almonds, hazelnuts, cocoa, baking powder, and salt, and mix on low until combined.

Divide the dough into two pieces. Press one half evenly into the bottom and up the sides of the prepared pan (1½ inches up the sides if you're using a springform pan). Roll out the other half between two sheets of parchment into a 12-inch circle. Refrigerate both for at least 30 minutes, or up to 2 days.

Remove the base from the refrigerator and fill it with the jam, smoothing the top with a small offset spatula.

Peel the top layer of parchment off the rolled-out dough, flip the dough over, and peel off the back layer. Cut half the dough into 1-inch-wide strips and half into ½-inch-wide strips. Starting at one edge of the pan, lay the strips ¾ inch apart, alternating thicknesses. Repeat on top, placing the strips perpendicular to the first layer, to make a lattice pattern. Refrigerate for at least 30 minutes or up to overnight.

Preheat the oven to 350°F (175°C).

Bake the tart for between 1 hour and 1 hour and 10 minutes, until the jam is bubbling and the edges are lightly browned. Let cool completely in the pan on a wire rack.

Unmold and serve with the whipped cream. The Linzertorte can be stored in an airtight container at room temperature for up to 3 days.

The fact that this looks like a giant Hostess Ho Hos is endlessly funny and delightful to me, but the flavors are actually quite sophisticated. A sponge flavored with rye flour and coffee is rolled around Black Currant & Sweet Cherry Jam along with whipped milk chocolate ganache. It's then bathed in a dark chocolate and crème de cassis glaze and finished with crunchy cocoa nibs. I know that all sounds like a lot, but it's pretty easy given how great this cake looks. I use Stella Parks's genius trick for rolling up sponge cake.

Coffee Swiss Roll with Whipped Milk Chocolate Ganache

Serves 10

For the Whipped Ganache:

100 g (3½ oz) milk chocolate pistoles

250 mL (1 cup) heavy cream

1 Tbsp light corn syrup

¼ tsp salt

For the Cake:

190 g (1⅓ cups) all-purpose flour

100 g (½ cup + 3 Tbsp) whole rye flour

1 tsp baking powder

½ tsp salt

125 mL (½ cup) strong coffee

58 g (¼ cup) melted unsalted butter

4 large eggs, at room temperature

200 g (1 cup) sugar

1 tsp vanilla extract

1½ jars Black Currant & Sweet Cherry Jam (page 96)

To make the ganache, place the chocolate in a heat-proof bowl. In a small pan, combine the cream, corn syrup, and salt, and bring to a boil over medium-high heat. Pour just enough of the cream mixture over the chocolate to cover it and wait 1 minute for it to melt. Do not stir while it's melting. Whisk the mixture until emulsified, and then whisk in the remaining cream mixture. Place plastic wrap directly on the surface of the ganache to stop a skin from forming and refrigerate until thoroughly chilled, at least 2 hours. This can be made up to 2 days in advance.

To make the cake, preheat the oven to 350°F (175°C). Grease a half sheet pan with butter or nonstick spray and line with parchment paper.

In a small bowl, combine both flours, the baking powder, and salt.

In a measuring cup, mix together the coffee and melted butter.

For the Glaze:

230 g (8 oz) dark chocolate pistoles

250 mL (1 cup) heavy cream

1 Tbsp butter

1 Tbsp light corn syrup

45 mL (3 Tbsp) crème de cassis

Cocoa nibs, for sprinkling (optional)

NOTE: *Can sub Black Forest Jam (page 172) (use kirsch instead of crème de cassis) or a good-quality store-bought black currant jam.*

In a stand mixer fitted with the whisk attachment, whip the eggs, sugar, and vanilla on medium-high speed until they reach the ribbon stage, when the mixture is pale and thick and leaves ribbon-like trails when lifted that take a moment to sink back in. With the mixer running on low, add one-third of the flour mixture, then half of the coffee mixture. Repeat until all is incorporated. Turn off the mixer. Using a spatula, gently fold the mixture to finish mixing. Pour into the prepared pan, spreading the batter evenly with an offset spatula.

Bake for 20 to 25 minutes, until the cake springs back when gently touched and a toothpick inserted in the center of the cake comes out with just a few moist crumbs attached.

Remove from the oven and, using oven mitts, immediately cover it tightly with aluminum foil. Place the pan on a wire rack and let cool to room temperature.

In a stand mixer fitted with the whisk attachment, whip the ganache on medium-high speed until it holds firm peaks.

Remove the foil from the cake. Using an offset spatula, spread the jam over the surface, leaving a 1-inch border along one of the short ends. Top with the whipped ganache, again leaving a 1-inch border. Starting at the short end without the border, begin to roll up the cake, peeling away the parchment as you go and using it to lift and roll the next section. Once the cake is rolled, wrap it tightly in parchment or plastic wrap and refrigerate, seam side down, for at least 1 hour, or up to overnight.

To make the glaze, place the chocolate in a heatproof bowl. In a small pot, combine the cream, butter, and corn syrup. Heat over medium-high, stirring to melt the butter. Once the mixture starts to boil, pour it over the chocolate. Wait 1 minute for it to melt. Do not stir while it's melting. Whisk the mixture until emulsified and then whisk in the crème de cassis. Let it cool for a few minutes, until it is thick but still pourable.

To assemble, remove the cake from the refrigerator and unwrap. Using a serrated knife, trim a little off either end to get a clean line.

Set a wire rack over a rimmed sheet pan and place the cake on top. Pour the glaze over top, using an offset spatula to make sure the cake is evenly covered, especially at the ends. Sprinkle with cocoa nibs, if using, transfer to a serving platter, and refrigerate, uncovered, until ready to serve.

This may seem like a slightly strange pairing, but we've known at least since the Sachertorte was introduced (c. 1832) that apricot and chocolate can play well together.

This is a particularly attractive jam, bright orange and dotted with black spots, like a cartoon cheetah. Anyone would be delighted to receive it as a gift.

Apricot & Cocoa Nib Jam

Makes four to five 250 mL (8 oz) jars

1.08 kg (6 cups) pitted apricots, cut into ½-inch pieces

475 g (2¼ cups + 2 Tbsp) sugar

115 g (⅓ cup) honey

60 mL (¼ cup) lemon juice

2 Tbsp cocoa nibs

In a large bowl, combine the apricots, sugar, honey, and lemon juice and let macerate for at least 15 minutes, or up to 1 week, covered, in the refrigerator.

Prepare the jars (see page 20).

Transfer the mixture to a pot or preserving pan. Heat on medium-high, stirring occasionally. When the mixture comes to a boil, add the cocoa nibs. Continue to boil hard, stirring frequently.

When the setting point is reached (see page 23), remove from the heat and ladle into the prepared jars to within ¼ to ⅛ inch of the rim. Remove any air bubbles, wipe the rims as necessary, seal, and invert 1 to 2 minutes. Flip right side up and let the jam sit, undisturbed, for 24 hours.

When it comes to brownies, there are two camps: chewy and fudgy. For the most part, I prefer chewy, and that's what these are, besides being shot through with milk chocolate and glossy apricot jam. But when I was testing the recipe, I accidentally doubled the amount of butter instead of reducing it as I had meant to. The result was so delicious it almost ended up beating these out for a place in this book. The double-butter brownies were densely fudgy, so much so that one friend mistook them for chocolate fudge. So if fudgy is your camp, just increase the butter to 200 grams (¾ cup + 2 tablespoons) and you'll be delighted. Either way, I like these cold, potentially with a glass of milk, in spite of generally never wanting a glass of milk. Brownies are funny that way.

Jam-Swirled Brownies

Makes 25 squares |

230 g (8 oz) dark chocolate

86 g (6 Tbsp) unsalted butter

200 g (1 cup) sugar

1 tsp vanilla extract

3 large eggs

70 g (½ cup) all-purpose flour

½ tsp flaky salt

65 g (2¼ oz) milk chocolate pistoles, divided

½ jar Apricot & Cocoa Nib Jam (page 103)

Preheat the oven to 350°F (175°C). Grease an 8-inch square pan with butter or nonstick spray and line with parchment paper.

In a small, sturdy pot over low heat, or in a bowl set over a pot of simmering water, or in the microwave in 20- to 30-second bursts, melt the chocolate and butter together. Set aside to cool slightly.

Stir in the sugar and vanilla. Then beat in the eggs one by one. Add the flour and salt and beat hard for at least 30 seconds, until the mixture is thick and glossy (if you under-beat it, you'll end up with a greasy slab!). Fold in half of the milk chocolate and then pour the mixture into the prepared pan. Drop teaspoons of jam onto the surface of the brownie, then scatter with the remaining milk chocolate pistoles.

NOTE: *Can sub Black Currant &
Sweet Cherry Jam (page 96), Black
Forest Jam (page 172), or a good-quality
store-bought apricot jam.*

Bake for about 35 minutes, until just set. Let cool completely before cutting (or refrigerate first for even cleaner cutting).

The brownies will keep in an airtight container in the refrigerator for at least 1 week.

I bring my grandmothers' old recipes up a lot because they are so important to me, almost like being able to ask my grandmothers questions about baking from beyond the grave. When I somehow misplaced my maternal grandmother's handwritten whipped shortbread recipe, I was totally devastated. I looked everywhere, but to no avail. So I began to try other recipes. Again and again, none were as light, as toothsome, or as buttery, and none of them seemed to hold their shape properly. Finally, I reached out to my aunts. When my aunt Sandra sent me the recipe, I recognized it at once. I cannot thank her enough!

If you don't own a piping bag and a star tip, you can roll these into balls instead, but they look so much more impressive piped. I encourage you to try!

Whipped Shortbread Thumbprints

Makes 32 cookies |

230 g (1 cup) unsalted butter, very soft

63 g (½ cup) icing sugar

½ tsp vanilla paste (optional)

210 g (1½ cups) all-purpose flour

32 g (¼ cup) cornstarch

½ tsp salt

⅓ jar Apricot & Cocoa Nib Jam (page 103)

Preheat the oven to 300°F (150°C). Line two baking sheets with parchment paper.

In a stand mixer fitted with the paddle attachment, beat together the butter and icing sugar on medium-high speed until pale and very creamy. Beat in the vanilla paste, if using. Add the flour, cornstarch, and salt and beat on low until combined, scraping down the sides to make sure everything is incorporated.

Transfer the dough to a piping bag fitted with a no. 5 star tip. Pipe rosettes onto the prepared baking sheets. Using a wet finger, make a depression in each rosette and then carefully fill each one with ½ teaspoon of jam.

Bake for about 20 minutes, until firm to the touch (they should be barely golden at most).

NOTES: *Can sub Summer Pudding Jam (page 154), Tutti Frutti Jam (page 185), or a good-quality store-bought apricot jam. These are also great without the jam, topped with an Amarena cherry or a slice of candied kumquat before baking.*

Cool on the pan on a wire rack.

The cookies will keep in an airtight container at room temperature for many weeks, although it seems highly unlikely considering how good they are. They can also be frozen, well wrapped, for up to 2 months.

[left to right] Cranberry & Clementine Jam (page 118), Pink Grapefruit & Toasted Almond Marmalade (page 111), and Dried Apricot & Verjus Butter (page 132)

This is my perfect childhood breakfast in a jar. Also, it's maybe the prettiest preserve in this book (or at least tied with Apricot & Cocoa Nib Jam, page 103). I came up with it ages ago as a tribute to a classic: a halved grapefruit, the segments often preemptively loosened from their membranes, covered in brown sugar and broiled until hot and bubbly. Brown sugar lends a bit of that burnt sugar flavor that's so delicious. Almonds seemed a perfect natural pairing with the grapefruit, but I realized recently they aren't featured in a traditionally boiled grapefruit recipe. Maybe I thought they would mimic the toasty flavor of the broiled top? No matter—it's very good marmalade.

Pink Grapefruit & Toasted Almond Marmalade

Makes six 250 mL (8 oz) jars

1.2 kg (3) pink grapefruits

800 g (4 cups) sugar

440 g (2 cups) brown sugar

125 mL (½ cup) lemon juice

45 g (⅓ cup) slivered almonds

Place the grapefruit in a pot large enough to hold them in a single layer. Cover them with water, cover the pot, and bring them to a boil over high heat. Turn down the heat to medium and simmer until they're very soft. It will take about 1 hour and 30 minutes. Let them cool in the water, preferably overnight.

Halve the cooled grapefruits, scoop out their insides, and run the flesh through the small disk of a food mill or push it through a sieve (the latter takes more elbow grease) set over a large bowl. This will collect all the delicious flesh and juice, leaving behind the chewy membranes. Quarter the emptied halves and slice the peel as thick as you like. I favor ¼-inch slices. Combine the sliced peel with both sugars and the lemon juice in the bowl containing the juice and flesh.

Preheat the oven to 300°F (150°C) or set a pan over medium heat. Toast the almonds until golden, about 7 minutes in the oven or 5 minutes in the pan. Set aside.

Prepare the jars (see page 20).

Transfer the grapefruit mixture to a pot or preserving pan. Heat on medium-high, stirring frequently. When the mixture comes to a boil, add the almonds. Continue to boil hard until the setting point is reached (see page 23). Pour into the prepared jars to within ¼ to ⅛ inch of the rim. Remove any air bubbles, wipe the rims if necessary, seal, and invert for 1 to 2 minutes. Flip right side up and let the jam sit, undisturbed, for 24 hours.

For me, Christmas is canceled if there are no mincemeat tarts. My granny made them when I was growing up, then my aunt Sue took over, and now I make them at home if I can't have Sue's. The thing is, hers are superlatively flaky and delicious, even when frozen and then thawed (which means you can make these a month in advance!). The secret, of course, is lard, but I still can't crack her code. Instead, I created a lard variation of my usual galette dough and made something that at least gets very close to hers. I've tried all sorts of mincemeat recipes, including the medieval way with meat, but this recipe uses brown butter, which is much nicer to make than it is to clean suet. This makes mincemeat for about 36 tarts, so you can triple the pastry recipe (they freeze well), or just make 12 tarts and know you have mincemeat in the refrigerator, which keeps well and is an exceptionally comforting thought.

Mincemeat Tarts

Makes 12 tarts |

For the Mincemeat:

550 g (3) apples

250 g (1 large) quince

165 g (¾ cup) brown sugar

100 g (¾ cup) currants

100 g (⅔ cup) golden raisins

85 g (½ cup) dried sour cherries

58 g (¼ cup) Brown Butter (page 228)

50 g (⅓ cup) diced candied ginger

50 g (¼ cup + 2 Tbsp) toasted sliced almonds

1½ tsp Mixed Spice (page 233)

Zest and juice of 1 orange

150 g (½ cup) Pink Grapefruit & Toasted Almond Marmalade (page 111), chopped

60 mL (¼ cup) brandy

To make the mincemeat, peel, core, and coarsely grate the apples and quince. Place them in a medium pot, along with the sugar, currants, raisins, cherries, butter, ginger, almonds, mixed spice, orange zest and juice, and marmalade. Heat on low, stirring occasionally, until the apples start to give off their juice. Increase the heat to medium and cook, stirring occasionally, until the dried fruit looks plump and the quince is pinkish and tender. This will take about 30 minutes. Remove from the heat, stir in the brandy, and let cool in the pot to room temperature. This will keep in an airtight container in the refrigerator for up to 2 months.

For the Tarts:

1 recipe Galette Dough (single crust, lard variation) (page 232)

Whole milk or Egg Wash (page 229) (optional)

NOTE: *Can sub any chunky marmalade to make the mincemeat.*

To make the tarts, let the galette dough sit at room temperature for about 10 minutes. Preheat the oven to 375°F (190°C). Grease a 12-cup muffin tin with butter or nonstick spray.

On a floured surface, roll out the dough to ⅛ inch thick. Using a 3½-inch plain cutter, cut out 12 rounds. Using a 2¾-inch plain cutter, cut out 12 more rounds. Fit the larger rounds snugly into the prepared muffin cups and fill each one with 2 scant tablespoons of mincemeat. Using a wet finger or pastry brush, moisten the edges and then top each one with a smaller pastry round, pressing gently to seal. Use a paring knife to make a small x in the top of each tart. For a more golden finish, brush the tops with milk or egg wash— my family doesn't and I'm sentimental, so I don't.

Bake the tarts for about 35 minutes, until golden brown and the mincemeat is bubbling up through the x. Cool for at least 20 minutes in the pan on a wire rack before using a mini offset spatula to help unmold them. Serve immediately or store, well wrapped, at room temperature for up to 3 days (reheat in a 325°F/160°C) oven for a few minutes before serving). These also freeze well in an airtight container or wrapped in aluminum foil lined with wax paper for up to 3 months.

I am very picky about muffins, as they are often either thinly disguised cakes or apparently related to cardboard. That means you can be sure these are real winners. They look very appealing, with their golden kamut hue and pink grapefruit supreme peeking out from under the polka-dot poppy seed streusel. They make an excellent breakfast or snack, boasting whole grain fiber and a little almond protein. But most importantly, they taste excellent. Go the extra mile and supreme the grapefruit (see page 41). With a little practice you'll be doing it with your eyes closed (that's an expression—don't handle a knife with your eyes closed).

Kamut & Poppyseed Muffins

Makes 12 muffins |

For the Streusel:

100 g (½ cup) sugar

70 g (½ cup) kamut flour

2 tsp poppy seeds

35 g (2½ Tbsp) unsalted butter, melted

Preheat the oven to 375°F (190°C). Place a 12-cup muffin tin on a half sheet pan and line with paper liners, preferably of the deep tulip variety.

To make the streusel, place the sugar, flour, poppy seeds, and butter in a small bowl and rub together with your fingertips until the mixture is sandy and clumpy. Reserve in the refrigerator or freezer until ready to use.

For the Muffins:

115 g (½ cup) unsalted butter, softened

150 g (¾ cup) sugar

1 tsp baking powder

½ tsp baking soda

½ tsp salt

1 grapefruit

2 large eggs, at room temperature

190 mL (¾ cup) buttermilk, at room temperature

105 g (⅓ cup) Pink Grapefruit & Toasted Almond Marmalade (page 111)

105 g (¾ cup) all-purpose flour

105 g (¾ cup) kamut flour

60 g (½ cup) ground almonds

1 Tbsp poppy seeds

NOTE: *Can sub Cranberry & Clementine Jam (page 118), A Different Seville Marmalade (page 70), or a good-quality store-bought chunky marmalade. Lemon or blood orange curd is excellent as well.*

To make the muffins, in a stand mixer fitted with the paddle attachment, add the butter, sugar, baking powder, baking soda, and salt. Use a grater to zest half the grapefruit into the bowl. Mix on medium speed until well combined. With the mixer running, add the eggs one at a time, mixing well between each addition. Scrape down the sides of the bowl with a spatula.

In a measuring cup, combine the buttermilk and marmalade.

Add both flours, the ground almonds, and poppy seeds to the butter and sugar mixture and mix on low. With the mixer running, gradually pour in the buttermilk mixture. Increase the speed to medium for 5 seconds just to make sure everything gets friendly.

Divide the batter evenly between the 12 muffin cups. Supreme the grapefruit (see page 41) and top each muffin with one segment. Sprinkle the streusel generously over the muffins.

Bake for about 30 minutes, until golden brown and a toothpick inserted in the center of a muffin comes out with just a few moist crumbs attached.

Cool in the pan on a wire rack for at least 15 minutes before eating. Good news, though—thanks to the ground almonds and marmalade, these stay tender for days and days if stored in an airtight container at room temperature.

I like this jam-marmalade hybrid because it looks like a holiday party in a jar. The cranberries, dressed in appropriately festive red, become translucent and glitter like jewels, while the strips of clementine peel resemble streamers or confetti. As a pair, they are elegant and will outlast the holiday overindulgence in their understated manner.

Cranberry & Clementine Jam

Makes six 250 mL (8 oz) jars

600 g (6–8) clementines
900 g (4½ cups) sugar
400 g (3½ cups) cranberries
125 mL (½ cup) lemon juice

NOTE: *You can add some warm spices or a few tablespoons of brandy at the end to turn up the holiday spirit.*

Place the clementines in a pot large enough to hold them in a single layer. Cover them with water, cover the pot, and bring to a boil over high heat. Turn down the heat to medium and simmer for about 45 minutes, until they are very soft. Let them cool in the water, preferably overnight.

In the meantime, combine the sugar, cranberries, and lemon juice in a large bowl and macerate, covered, overnight.

The next day, prepare the jars (see page 20).

Transfer the clementines from their bath to a cutting board. Remove any stem ends and then quarter the fruit and cut them into ¼-inch-thick slices.

Place the macerated cranberry mixture in a pot or preserving pan and add the clementine slices. Heat on medium-high and bring to a hard boil, stirring frequently. When the setting point is reached (see page 23), remove from the heat and fill the prepared jars to within ¼ to ⅛ inch of the rim. Remove any air bubbles, wipe the rims if necessary, seal, and invert for 1 to 2 minutes. Flip right side up and let the jam sit, undisturbed, for 24 hours.

Recipe pictured on page 110

If you're starting to get the idea that I like meringue, fruit, and cream, then you've got me pegged. If you feel the same way, this one's for you. When I was growing up, pavlova often showed up as a base to showcase beautiful summer fruit, and it's a great vehicle for that to be sure. But what a blessed sight after a rich midwinter meal! It's a light, airy dessert, sharp and bright with the bounty of citrus that is winter's saving grace. What's more, it's extremely easy to make, yet has a very celebratory air about it, plus it'll ward off scurvy. What more could you possibly ask from a dessert?

Wintertime Pavlova

Serves 6 to 8

For the Base:

120 g (4) egg whites, at room temperature

Pinch of salt

250 g (1¼ cups) sugar

1 tsp cornstarch

1 tsp vanilla extract

1 tsp vinegar (preferably white wine)

Preheat the oven to 300°F (150°C). Line a half sheet pan with parchment paper.

In a stand mixer fitted with the whisk attachment, whip the egg whites with the salt on medium-high speed until they begin to hold soft peaks. With the mixer running, gradually add the sugar. Continue to beat until the meringue is glossy and stiff. Fold in the cornstarch, vanilla, and vinegar.

Transfer the meringue to the prepared pan and spread into a serving plate–sized oval, making a large depression in the center where the filling will go. Bake for 1 hour, until firm, then turn off the oven, prop open the door a little, and let cool completely inside. When cool, transfer to a serving platter or cutting board.

For the Topping:

1.2 kg (6–8) mixed citrus fruit

½ jar Cranberry & Clementine Jam (page 118)

250 mL (1 cup) heavy cream

125 g (½ cup) sour cream

2 Tbsp icing sugar

1 Tbsp orange liqueur (such as Grand Marnier) or 1 tsp vanilla paste

Handful of pomegranate arils, to garnish

NOTE: *Can sub A Different Seville Marmalade (page 70) or any good-quality store-bought marmalade.*

If your citrus mix includes grapefruit, oranges, and lemons, supreme (page 41) them. If you're using thinner-skinned fruits, like clementines, peel and slice them into wheels. Place a sieve over a bowl, and place the citrus in the sieve to drain off any excess juice (reserve the juice for another use). In another bowl, whisk the jam to liquefy it and then fold in the drained citrus pieces.

In a stand mixer fitted with the whisk attachment, whip the cream, sour cream, and icing sugar on medium-high speed until the mixture holds firm peaks. Beat in the orange liqueur to combine.

Spread the cream over the meringue base, leaving a border all the way around, and top with the citrus mixture. Sprinkle with pomegranate arils and serve.

The meringue can be made a few days ahead if protected from humidity in the interim, but it is best assembled just before serving. Any leftovers can be stored, covered, in the refrigerator overnight and are frankly pretty easy to eat the next day.

The problem with cinnamon buns is that I don't like cinnamon. There, I said it. I would much rather have these, which have the same squidgy, sweet, buttery, yeasty pleasure to them, but punctuated by tart, bright cranberry and clementine instead of the usual, insipid suspect. They are much prettier on a winter's day as well—pink! orange!—like a sunrise, which I think we can all agree is the most apt color for a morning bun. These are so good, in fact, that my multitalented friend Merida Anderson crafted a miniature version to forever immortalize them (see page 122), really bringing my love of baking and miniatures to a whole new apex.

Morning Buns

Makes 9 buns

For the Buns:

80 mL (⅓ cup) milk

2 tsp active dry yeast

1 orange

77 g (⅓ cup) unsalted butter, melted

1 egg, at room temperature

45 g (3 Tbsp) sour cream

38 g (3 Tbsp) sugar

½ tsp salt

280 g (2 cups) all-purpose flour, divided

1 Tbsp unsalted butter, softened

1 jar Cranberry & Clementine Jam (page 118)

Heat the milk in a small saucepan to just warm, 100°F to 110°F (38°C to 43°C). Whisk in the yeast and let stand for 5 minutes, until foamy.

Zest half the orange.

In a stand mixer fitted with the whisk attachment, whip together the zest, butter, egg, sour cream, sugar, and salt on medium-high speed. When the yeast mixture is ready, add it to the bowl and fit the mixer with the dough hook. Add half the flour and mix on low until incorporated. With the mixer running on low, gradually add the rest of the flour and then mix on medium-high for about 10 minutes to knead. (Or knead it by hand for 15 to 20 minutes.) The dough should be smooth and bouncy. Grease a large bowl with butter, add the dough, cover, and let rise in a warm, draft-free place until doubled in volume. This will take about 1 hour (or you can let it rise in the refrigerator overnight).

For the Glaze:

125 g (1 cup) icing sugar

20 g (1½ Tbsp) unsalted butter, melted

1 Tbsp Cranberry & Clementine Jam (page 118)

1 Tbsp orange juice (from reserved orange)

NOTE: *Can sub Strawberry & Passion Fruit Jam (page 84), Dried Apricot & Verjus Butter (page 132), Prune & Meyer Lemon Butter (page 145), or a good-quality store-bought marmalade.*

Grease an 8-inch square pan with butter or nonstick spray and line with parchment paper.

On a floured surface, pat down the dough and roll it into a 10- x 12-inch rectangle, ensuring even thickness. Spread the soft butter over the surface of the dough (I like to do this with my fingers), then use a mini offset spatula to evenly spread the jam over the dough, leaving a 1-inch border along one long end. Starting at the long end without the border, roll up the dough into a log, pinching the seam to seal. Use a serrated knife to cut the log into nine evenly sized slices. Place the slices, three by three, in the prepared pan. Cover with plastic wrap and loosely drape with a tea towel. Let it rise in a warm, draft-free place until puffy. This will take about 30 minutes. (Or wrap the dough and pan in plastic and let it rise in the refrigerator overnight. Bring to room temperature before proceeding.)

Preheat the oven to 375°F (190°C).

Bake for 30 to 35 minutes, until golden and an instant read thermometer inserted into the center of a bun reads 210°F (99°C). Let cool in the pan on a wire rack for 20 minutes before glazing.

To make the glaze, whisk together the icing sugar, butter, jam, and orange juice. Pour the glaze evenly over the buns. Let it set for about 30 minutes before serving, or be okay with getting sticky and eat immediately.

These are best eaten within a few hours of being made but can be reheated, wrapped in foil, in a 300°F (150°C) oven to revive them the next day.

This is a great wintertime or early spring jam, both times when not much jam making is usually happening. Fortunately, it's when mangoes are at their best (and cheapest). I liked the yellow-fleshed Ataulfo mangoes the most when I created this, but more and more I'm finding gorgeous mangoes from all over the world that vie for my affections at the grocery store.

Sea buckthorn berries are easiest to find frozen. Trust me, they are worth tracking down (you can likely find them at your local specialty food store). I like to call them the passion fruit of the north, as they are native to Canada, Russia, Mongolia, and northern Europe. They match the vibrant color of the mango and add both seedy texture and a peerless musky acidity.

Mango & Sea Buckthorn Jam

Makes four 250 mL (8 oz) jars

775 g (3⅔ cups) peeled and chopped (½-inch pieces) mango

425 g (3 cups) sea buckthorn berries

600 g (3 cups) sugar

60 mL (¼ cup) lemon juice

In a large bowl, combine the mango and sea buckthorn with the sugar and lemon juice. Let macerate for at least 15 minutes, or up to 1 week, covered, in the refrigerator.

Prepare the jars (see page 20).

Transfer the mixture to a pot or preserving pan. Heat on medium-high and bring to a hard boil, stirring frequently.

When the setting point is reached (see page 23), remove from the heat. Ladle into the prepared jars to within ¼ to ⅛ inch of the rim. Remove any air bubbles, wipe the rims if necessary, seal, and invert for 1 to 2 minutes. Flip right side up and let the jam sit, undisturbed, for 24 hours.

Rifling through my grandmothers' clippings, I was intrigued by a recipe called Lime Pots de Crème. I whisked together the sweetened condensed milk with egg yolks and used mango purée instead of lime juice. I poured it into ramekins to chill, and it was . . . weird, even without the sour cream topping. Too smooth somehow? Undaunted, I decided it seemed like a pie filling and poured the next round into a graham cracker crust. It was . . . ok. Finally I realized I was basically making key lime pie but with mango, and the real key to success was to bake it for a firmer filling to contrast with the crisp crust and soft, whipped sour cream (a nod to the original). It was . . . perfection. If you can find it, sea buckthorn juice (or purée) instead of lime juice really brings it all together, and if you have some sea buckthorn berries hanging around they would make a pretty cute garnish.

Mango Cream Pie

Makes one 9-inch pie |

For the Crust:

170 g (1½ cups) graham cracker crumbs

86 g (6 Tbsp) unsalted butter, melted

50 g (¼ cup) sugar

For the Filling:

80 g (4) egg yolks

1 (14 oz/397 g) can sweetened condensed milk

160 g (½ cup + 2 Tbsp) mango purée

2 Tbsp lime juice or sea buckthorn juice

¼ tsp salt

¼ tsp citric acid (optional)

½ jar Mango & Sea Buckthorn Jam (page 125)

Preheat the oven to 350°F (175°C). Grease a 9-inch pie plate with butter or nonstick spray.

To make the crust, in a bowl, mix together the graham cracker crumbs, melted butter, and sugar. Press the mixture evenly into the pie plate, making sure it goes right up the sides. Bake for 10 minutes, then let cool in the pan on a wire rack.

To make the filling, in a large bowl whisk the yolks with the condensed milk until well combined. Whisk in the mango purée and juice, followed by the salt and citric acid. Pour this mixture into the crust and dot it with spoonfuls of jam. Using the point of a knife, gently swirl in the jam. Bake for 25 to 30 minutes, until set. Let cool completely in the pan on a wire rack. Once cooled, refrigerate, uncovered, for at least 2 hours, or up to overnight.

To Finish:

250 mL (1 cup) heavy cream

125 g (½ cup) sour cream

2 Tbsp icing sugar

Whole sea buckthorn, for garnish
(optional)

———————

NOTE: *Can sub Dark & Stormy Marmalade (page 221) (sub lime juice for the mango purée) or a good-quality store-bought mango jam or butter.*

———————

Just before serving, in a stand mixer fitted with the whisk attachment, whip the cream with the sour cream and icing sugar on medium-high speed until firm peaks form. Spread the cream artfully on the top of the chilled pie and decorate with sea buckthorn berries, if using.

Any leftovers can be stored in the refrigerator, covered, for up to 2 days.

As you can imagine, writing a dessert cookbook means that one's home is overtaken by cakes, tarts, cookies, and ice creams. While this sounds in some ways like a dream come true, it's just not humanly possible for two people to eat that many sweets. So I pawned off as many desserts as I possibly could—leaving them in the foyer for my neighbors, sending them to work with my partner, showing up at dinner parties with three or four desserts, forcing houseguests to eat donuts for breakfast and pie for lunch . . . As sweet-fatigued as I was, however, this dacquoise was one dessert I just couldn't leave alone, sneaking bites of it any time of day.

If you've never had dacquoise, well, it's just meringue with coconut or nuts in it, so no big deal. And if you've never eaten a buttercream with a crème anglaise base, prepare to have your mind blown.

Coconut & Mango Dacquoise

Serves 8 to 10

For the Dacquoise:

180 g (6) egg whites, at room temperature

½ tsp salt

225 g (1 cup + 2 Tbsp) sugar

175 g (1¾ cups) unsweetened desiccated coconut

2 Tbsp cornstarch

1 tsp vanilla extract

To make the dacquoise, preheat the oven to 300°F (150°C). Use the base of a springform pan to trace three 8½-inch circles onto parchment paper. Place one circle on a half sheet pan and two on a three-quarter sheet pan.

In a stand mixer fitted with the whisk attachment, whip the egg whites and salt on medium-high speed until they begin to hold soft peaks. With the mixer running, gradually add the sugar. Continue to whip until the mixture is glossy and holds stiff peaks. Fold in the coconut, cornstarch, and vanilla.

Divide the mixture evenly between the three circles and use a mini offset spatula to spread them evenly.

Bake for about 1 hour, rotating the sheets halfway through, until golden brown and dry. Let cool completely on the pan on a wire rack.

For the Buttercream:

190 mL (¾ cup) coconut milk

100 g (5) egg yolks

67 g (⅓ cup) sugar

290 g (1¼ cups) unsalted butter, softened

128 g (½ cup) mango purée

¼ tsp salt

To Assemble:

½ jar Mango & Sea Buckthorn Jam (page 125)

NOTE: *Can sub Dark & Stormy Marmalade (page 221) or a good-quality store-bought mango jam or butter.*

To make the buttercream, in a small pot over medium heat, heat the coconut milk just until it simmers.

In the meantime, in a bowl, whisk the egg yolks by hand with the sugar. Slowly whisk in the hot coconut milk then return the mixture to the pot. Cook, stirring constantly with a flexible spatula, until the mixture thickens slightly and an instant read thermometer reads 180°F (82°C), or the mixture coats the back of a spoon. Immediately remove from the heat and pour through a fine mesh sieve into a stand mixer fitted with the whisk attachment.

Whip the crème anglaise on high speed until cool. This will take 5 to 10 minutes. Turn down the speed to medium and add the butter 1 tablespoon at a time. Don't worry if the mixture looks broken—just turn the speed back up to high and whip until the mixture is glossy and creamy. Stop the mixer and add the mango purée and salt. Mix on low until incorporated then increase the speed again and mix until light and fluffy.

To assemble, place one disk of dacquoise on a serving platter. Heap on one-third of the buttercream and, using a mini offset spatula, spread it evenly over the disk. Dot half of the jam on top of the buttercream and spread it lightly and evenly. Repeat with the second disk of dacquoise, saving a spoonful of jam to decorate, if you like.

Place the last disk of dacquoise on top. Spread the remaining buttercream over the top layer, making attractive whorls and waves.

Serve immediately, or refrigerate for up to 3 days loosely covered. If it's refrigerated, bring it to room temperature at least 20 minutes before serving.

The verjus melon candy from *Brooks Headley's Fancy Desserts* (page 235) inspired this fruit butter. Brooks soaks dried fruit in verjus, the acidic juice of unripened grapes, to make a sort of candy. I soak dried apricots in Niagara verjus (available at your local food specialty store or online), purée them, and cook them down into a fruit butter. I actually sent him a jar of my jam in a classic fangirl move, but I don't think he ever got it. I've met him a few times subsequently but I've always been too shy to ask.

 ## Dried Apricot & Verjus Butter

Makes four 250 mL (8 oz) jars

450 g (2 cups) dried apricots (see note)

315 mL (scant 1¼ cups + 1 Tbsp) verjus, divided

600 mL (scant 2½ cups) water

600 g (3 cups) sugar

NOTE: *If you can, use dried Blenheim apricots, which have a far superior flavor. If not, this is equally delicious with the more readily available Turkish apricots. A verjus bath can do wonders.*

Recipe pictured on page 110

Using kitchen scissors, cut the apricots into quarters. In a medium bowl, combine the apricots and the 300 mL (scant 1¼ cups) of verjus. Cover and soak overnight at room temperature.

The next day, prepare the jars (see page 20).

The apricots should now be very plump, having absorbed nearly all the liquid. Using a blender, purée the apricots, thinning the mixture with some of the water if necessary. Transfer the purée to a pot or preserving pan and add the remaining water and the sugar. Heat on medium-high and bring to a boil, stirring frequently. Gradually lower the heat as the mixture thickens and sputters.

When the setting point is reached (it's a little different for a butter—see page 26), remove from the heat and add the remaining 15 mL (1 tablespoon) of verjus. Ladle into the prepared jars to within ¼ inch of the rim. Remove any air bubbles, wipe the rims if necessary, and seal fingertip-tight (just until you feel resistance).

Heat-process the butter for 10 minutes (see page 21).

My paternal grandmother was an incredible baker who specialized in European cakes like Dobos torte even when, according to my dad, she didn't own so much as a whisk. Frankly, at every gathering she brought her cakes to they blew every other dessert out of the water. I curse myself for having learned barely any of her recipes. After her death, I took as many of her old recipe clippings and notes as I could and found among them a handwritten Sachertorte recipe, which was where I started when creating this one. This is a classic Viennese coffeehouse cake, so I suggest you serve it with coffee and more unsweetened whipped cream than you think polite.

Sachertorte

Makes one 8-inch cake, serves 8 to 10 |

For the Cake:

115 g (4 oz) dark chocolate

100 g (7 Tbsp) unsalted butter, softened

94 g (¾ cup) icing sugar, divided

100 g (5) egg yolks

½ tsp vanilla extract

90 g (¾ cup) ground almonds

26 g (3 Tbsp) all-purpose flour

120 g (4) egg whites, at room temperature

Preheat the oven to 350°F (175°C). Grease an 8½-inch round springform pan with butter or nonstick spray and line the bottom with parchment paper.

In a small heatproof bowl set over a pan of simmering water, or in the microwave in 20- to 30-second bursts, melt the chocolate. Set aside to cool slightly.

In a stand mixer fitted with the paddle attachment, cream the butter with all but 2 tablespoons of the icing sugar on medium-high speed until light and fluffy. Add the egg yolks, one by one, mixing between each addition, followed by the vanilla. Add the melted chocolate and mix until well blended. Using a spatula, fold in the ground almonds and flour.

For the Filling and Glaze:

½ jar Dried Apricot & Verjus Butter
(page 132)

190 mL (¾ cup) heavy cream

1 Tbsp dark rum

1 Tbsp honey

172 g (6 oz) dark chocolate pistoles

Unsweetened, softly whipped cream,
for serving

NOTE: *Can sub Apricot &
Cocoa Nib Jam (page 103) or
a good-quality, smooth, store-
bought apricot jam.*

In a clean bowl, whisk the egg whites until frothy.
Add the remaining 2 tablespoons of icing sugar and
continue to whisk until stiff peaks form. Fold one-
third of the egg whites into the chocolate mixture to
lighten it, then gently fold in the remaining whites.

Scrape the mixture into the prepared pan, smoothing
the top. Bake for 45 to 50 minutes, until a toothpick
inserted into the center comes out with just a few
moist crumbs attached.

Cool for 10 minutes in the pan on a wire rack.
Remove the sides of the pan, then invert the cake onto
the rack, remove the bottom, and peel off the parchment. Let cool completely.

When it's cool, use a long serrated knife to cut the cake
into two layers. Evenly spread the bottom layer all the
way to the edges with most of the apricot butter. Place
the second layer on top, then coat the entire cake and
sides with a thin layer of the remaining apricot butter.

To make the glaze, in a small pot over medium-high
heat, heat the cream, rum, and honey. Place the chocolate in a heatproof bowl. When the cream comes to a
boil, pour it over top the chocolate. Leave the mixture
for 1 minute to melt undisturbed. Whisk until smooth.

Set the cake over a wire rack with a rimmed cookie sheet
underneath. Pour the glaze over the cake, using an offset
spatula to help it flow evenly over the sides. If your
kitchen is cool, you can let it set where it is. Otherwise,
carefully transfer the cake to a serving platter and refrigerate for at least 30 minutes to let the glaze set.

Serve slices accompanied by a mound of unsweetened
whipped cream and a cup of strong coffee.

The first time I tried making this idea come alive, I used whole spelt flour and half the amount of butter, before coming to my senses and making it less austere. This is an excellent breakfast or afternoon snack. My partner thinks these buns are reminiscent of almond croissants, while for me they invoke the Chinese cocktail buns that I discovered as a child and remain a favorite to this day. Nothing wrong with a hybrid of those two treats, I say!

Apricot & Almond Tea Buns

Makes 12 buns

172 g (¾ cup) dried apricots

90 mL (¼ cup + 2 Tbsp) amaretto

190 mL (¾ cup) whole milk

2 Tbsp active dry yeast

525 g (3¾ cups) all-purpose flour, divided

230 g (1 cup) unsalted butter, softened

3 large eggs, at room temperature

100 g (½ cup) sugar

1¼ tsp salt

½ tsp almond extract

½ tsp vanilla paste

60 g (¼ cup) marzipan or almond paste

¼ jar Dried Apricot & Verjus Butter (page 132)

1 recipe Egg Wash (page 229)

90 g (⅔ cup) sliced almonds

Icing sugar, for dusting

Dice the dried apricots. Warm the amaretto in a small pot on low heat, then add the apricots and let cool. They will absorb almost all of the liquid. This will take about 1 hour.

Heat the milk in a small saucepan to just warm, 100°F to 110°F (38°C to 43°C). Whisk in the yeast and let stand for 5 minutes, until foamy.

In a stand mixer fitted with the dough hook, mix together the yeast mixture, half of the flour, the butter, eggs, sugar, salt, almond extract, and vanilla paste on low speed until combined. Add the remaining flour and mix on low again. When the flour is fully incorporated, increase the speed to medium and let the mixer knead the dough for 5 to 10 minutes, until it is smooth and elastic and pulls away from the sides of the bowl. Add the soaked apricots and any remaining soaking liquid and mix briefly until just combined.

NOTE: *Can sub Damson Jam (page 57), Cranberry & Clementine Jam (page 118), or a good-quality store-bought apricot jam.*

Grease a large bowl with butter or nonstick spray, add the dough, cover with plastic wrap and a tea towel, and leave in a warm, draft-free place to rise until doubled in size. This will take between 1 hour and 1 hour and 30 minutes. (Or put the dough in the refrigerator to rise slowly overnight and bring to room temperature before proceeding.)

Preheat the oven to 350°F (175°C). Line a baking sheet with parchment paper.

Divide the dough into 12 evenly sized pieces. Roll each into a ball and place under a tea towel. Grab a ball, flatten it, and place 1 teaspoon each of the marzipan and apricot butter in the center. Gather in the edges of the dough and pinch them together, then flip the piece seam side down and form your hand into a claw to roll it into a ball with good surface tension; it will look taut and hold its shape. Repeat with the remaining dough, then place the buns, spaced a few inches apart, on the prepared sheet. Cover with plastic wrap and a tea towel and let rise in a warm, draft-free place until doubled in size. This will take about 40 minutes.

Brush the buns with the egg wash and sprinkle liberally with the sliced almonds.

Bake for 25 to 30 minutes, until golden brown and an instant read thermometer inserted in the center of a bun reads 210°F (99°C). Let cool on the pan on a wire rack for 15 minutes. Dust with a little icing sugar before serving.

This marmalade was inspired by my favorite, slightly obscure childhood ice cream, tiger tail. I'm not sure swirled orange and black licorice ice cream (like tiger stripes, get it?) was for every kid, but it hit all the right notes for me.

Le Tigre Marmalade

Makes four 250 mL (8 oz) jars

925 g (7–8) tangerines

900 g (4½ cups) sugar

100 mL (7 Tbsp) lemon juice

1¼ tsp ground star anise

Place the tangerines in a pot that fits them in a single layer and cover generously with water. Cover the pot with a lid, bring the water to a boil, then turn down the heat to medium and simmer until very soft. This will take about 1 hour. Remove from the heat and let them cool in the water, preferably overnight.

The next day, prepare the jars (see page 20).

Halve the tangerines, scoop out their insides, and run the flesh through the small disk of a food mill or push it through a mesh sieve. Keep all of the juice and pulp, and discard the membranes and any seeds.

Remove the stem end nubs from the peels and slice them into thin ribbons. Transfer to a wide, heavy-bottomed pan, and combine with the pulp, sugar, lemon juice, and star anise. Bring to a boil over medium-high heat. Cook at a rolling boil, stirring frequently (don't stray too far—this boiled over on me once!), until the setting point is reached (see page 23).

Remove from the heat and pour into the prepared jars to within ¼ to ⅛ inch of the rim. Wipe the rims if necessary, seal, and invert for 1 to 2 minutes. Flip right side up and let the jam sit, undisturbed, for 24 hours.

These days there are so many gorgeous, showstopping Bundt pans on the market that you could probably fill them with mashed potatoes and everyone would still be impressed (in fact, some people might prefer it). Fortunately, this cake has a flavor every bit as impressive as whatever pan you bake it in, plus it keeps for days, so get out your calendar and start making some coffee dates.

Tiger Pound Cake

Makes 1 Bundt, 12 to 16 servings |

86 g (3 oz) dark chocolate

292 g (2¼ cups) cake flour

1½ tsp baking powder

¾ tsp salt

¾ tsp ground star anise

1 jar Le Tigre Marmalade (page 139)

60 mL (¼ cup) heavy cream

230 g (1 cup) unsalted butter, softened

200 g (1 cup) sugar

4 large eggs, at room temperature

Zest of 1 orange

2 Tbsp vanilla extract

2 Tbsp cocoa powder

Icing sugar, for serving

NOTE: *Can sub A Different Seville Marmalade (page 70) or a good-quality store-bought marmalade.*

Preheat the oven to 350°F (175°C). Grease a 10-cup Bundt pan. For more intricately designed pans, use nonstick spray if possible. Otherwise, grease the pan very well with melted butter (use a pastry brush), coat with flour, tap out any excess flour, and refrigerate the pan until the batter is ready.

Melt the chocolate in a heatproof bowl set over a pot of simmering water, or in the microwave in 20- to 30-second bursts, and set aside to cool slightly.

Sift the flour, baking powder, salt, and ground star anise into a medium bowl.

In a measuring cup, combine the marmalade and cream.

In a stand mixer fitted with the paddle attachment, beat the butter on medium speed until creamy. Gradually add the sugar. Once all the sugar has been added, increase the speed to medium-high and beat until the mixture is pale and fluffy. Turn down the speed to medium and add the eggs, one by one, scraping down the bowl a few times. Mix in the orange zest and vanilla.

With the mixer running on low speed, add one-third of the flour mixture, followed by one-half of the marmalade mixture. Repeat until all is incorporated. Increase the speed to medium-high for 15 seconds to finish.

Pour half the batter into a clean bowl and add the melted chocolate and cocoa powder. Transfer to the prepared pan and top with the remaining batter.

Bake for about 1 hour, until the cake is golden brown and pulling away from the sides of the pan, and a toothpick inserted in the center of the cake comes out with just a few moist crumbs attached.

Let cool in the pan on a wire rack for 20 minutes before unmolding and letting it cool completely. Dust with a little icing sugar before serving.

My partner Kat studied abroad in Ireland for a year. The first time I went to visit was in the weeks just before Easter, when the Marks & Sparks was loaded with every possible variation of hot cross bun. We bought them all. That's a fond memory, but of course they are better homemade, and I developed the recipe the next year on Canadian soil to fill the void. Your whole kitchen will have the scent of spice, and you can eat them all squishy and hot, and toast and slather them with butter the next day. I think you should eat one of these traditional Easter treats each day for the whole month of April. This recipe in particular, of course.

Hot Cross Buns

Makes 12 buns |

For the Buns:

54 g (⅓ cup) golden raisins

58 g (⅓ cup) currants

165 mL (⅔ cup) whole milk

545 g (3¾ cups + 2 Tbsp) all-purpose flour

2 Tbsp sugar

4 tsp instant dry yeast

2 tsp Mixed Spice (page 233)

¾ tsp kosher salt

3 large eggs, at room temperature

165 mL (⅔ cup) Le Tigre Marmalade (page 139), coarsely chopped

115 g (½ cup) unsalted butter, softened

In a heatproof bowl, cover the raisins and currants with boiling water. Set aside to plump at room temperature.

Heat the milk to just warm in a small saucepan, 100°F to 110°F (38°C to 43°C).

In a stand mixer fitted with the dough hook, mix the warm milk with the flour, sugar, yeast, mixed spice, salt, eggs, marmalade, and butter on low speed until combined. Increase the speed to medium and let the machine knead the dough until it is smooth and elastic. This will take about 5 minutes.

Drain the raisins and currants and fold them into the dough by hand. Cover the bowl with plastic wrap and a tea towel, and set aside in a warm, draft-free place to rise until doubled in size. This will take about 1 hour and 30 minutes. (Or put the dough in the refrigerator to rise overnight and bring to room temperature before proceeding.)

For the Cross Paste:

26 g (3 Tbsp) all-purpose flour

Pinch of salt

½ tsp neutral oil

For the Glaze:

⅓ jar marmalade, preferably
A Different Seville Marmalade
(page 70)

NOTES: *Can sub Pink Grapefruit &
Toasted Almond Marmalade (page 111)
or any chunky marmalade (homemade or
store-bought), really, for the buns. You
can also bake the buns in a 9- x 13-inch
pan for the soft-sided pull-apart effect.*

Preheat the oven to 350°F (175°C). Line a sheet pan with parchment paper or grease a 9- x 13-inch pan with butter or nonstick spray.

On a lightly floured surface, divide the dough into 12 evenly sized pieces. Roll each into a ball and place them, a few inches apart, on the baking sheet. Cover with plastic wrap and a tea towel and let rise in a warm, draft-free place until doubled in size. This will take about 45 minutes.

In the meantime, in a small bowl, make the cross paste by whisking the flour, salt, and oil with 45 mL (3 tablespoons) of water. Just before baking the buns, transfer the cross paste to a piping bag fitted with a small tip and pipe crosses onto the buns.

Bake for 30 minutes, until golden brown.

To make the glaze, heat the marmalade in a small pot over medium heat until liquefied. Strain through a fine mesh sieve, discarding any peel. While the buns are still hot, brush them generously with the glaze.

I hope you like prunes! I think the cuisine of Eastern Europe gives them the best treatment, cooking them down into a thick paste to stuff into donuts. This butter recipe gives them a white wine bath and a dose of Meyer lemon zest and juice to bring a little acidity into the mix. It may not be much to look at, but this is honestly one of the most delicious things I've ever made.

 # Prune & Meyer Lemon Butter

Makes four to five 250 mL (8 oz) jars

800 g (5 cups) pitted prunes

1 (750 mL) bottle dry white wine

Zest of 3 Meyer lemons

Zest of 1 regular lemon

Juice of 2 Meyer lemons

250 g (1¼ cups) sugar

In a large bowl, combine the prunes and wine with all the lemon zest and juice. Cover and let sit at room temperature overnight.

The next day, prepare the jars (see page 20).

In a large pot or preserving pan, add the sugar to the prune mixture and mix to combine. Heat on medium-high, stirring, until the sugar is dissolved. Depending on how chunky you want your preserve to be, you can either let the prunes partially break down on their own or use a hand mixer to make a purée. I like something between chunky and smooth.

Continue to cook, stirring and turning down the heat as the mixture thickens and sputters, until thick and jammy (page 26).

Remove from the heat and ladle into the prepared jars to within ¼ inch of the rim. Remove any air bubbles, wipe the rims, and seal fingertip-tight (just until you feel resistance).

Recipe pictured on page 146

Heat-process for 10 minutes (see page 21).

Prune & Meyer Lemon Butter (page 145) and Buchty (pictured right)

I adored buchty when I was growing up. It was one of my paternal grandmother's specialties. I was recently reminded that in Czech, *buchty* just means buns, but they are so much more than that. My grandmother's were a rich dough, often filled with her homemade black currant jam, and tasted almost donut-like on account of the butter with which she doused the raised buns right before they went in the oven. After she passed away, I felt very disappointed that I'd never gotten the recipe, and for years I thought it was lost. I tried other recipes for buchty, but none matched hers. Then, one day, while I was going through a pile of her recipe clippings I'd inherited, I was overjoyed to find her handwritten recipe. It took a little decoding (there were not a lot of details, let me tell you), but I think I got it. I fill mine with prune butter as a nod to the Polish donuts I loved in Montreal, but you can try them with black currant or anything else that you might imagine would be delicious inside butter-doused enriched dough.

Buchty

Makes 16 buns |

250 mL (1 cup) whole milk, divided

1 envelope active dry yeast

50 g (¼ cup) + 1½ tsp sugar, divided, plus more for serving

115 g (½ cup) unsalted butter

¼ tsp salt

1 egg, lightly beaten

Zest of ½ lemon

350 g (2½ cups) flour

½ jar Prune & Meyer Lemon Butter (page 145)

115 g (½ cup) unsalted butter, melted

Heat 60 mL (¼ cup) of the milk to just warm in a small saucepan, 100°F to 110°F (38°C to 43°C).

In a stand mixer fitted with the dough attachment, use a spatula to combine the milk, yeast, and 1½ teaspoons of the sugar by hand. Let stand until the mixture is foamy, about 10 minutes.

In the meantime, in a medium pan on medium heat, combine the remaining milk and sugar with the butter and salt. Stir until the butter has melted. Remove from the heat and let cool to lukewarm, then add to the yeast mixture and mix on low to combine. Add the egg, lemon zest, and then the flour. Mix on medium-low speed until the dough is shiny and pliable. This will take 10 to 15 minutes. If the dough is sticky, little by little add up to 70 grams (½ cup) more flour.

Grease a bowl with butter or nonstick spray, add the dough, cover with plastic wrap and a tea towel, and let rise in a warm, draft-free spot until doubled in size. This will take about 1 hour. (Or let the dough rise in the refrigerator overnight and bring it to room temperature before proceeding.)

Grease an 8-inch square pan with butter.

Punch down the dough and turn it out onto a floured countertop. Pat it into a 12-inch square, then use a knife or a dough scraper to cut it into 16 squares. Place ½ tablespoon of prune and lemon butter in the center of each square, then one by one, carefully fold the dough around the filling, forming a ball. Place the filled balls of dough seam side up in the prepared pan in four rows of four. Cover with buttered plastic wrap and a tea towel, and let rise in a warm, draft-free place for 30 minutes.

Preheat the oven to 375°F (190°C). Set a wire rack over a rimmed baking sheet.

Remove the towel and plastic wrap from the pan, then pour the melted butter evenly over the buchty. Bake for 25 to 30 minutes, until the buchty are golden brown. Let cool in the pan on a wire rack for 5 minutes, then turn out onto the wire rack and sprinkle with sugar.

Serve warm or at room temperature.

Buchty are best eaten the day they are made, but if you eat them the next day, wrap them in aluminum foil and heat them in a 300°F (150°C) oven for 10 to 15 minutes to warm them up.

These resemble a familiar childhood treat but are actually an alchemical miracle. They have to be one of the best things I've ever made. Something about the sweet prune–earthy rye–bitter coffee–flaky butter–perfectly salted combo is beyond magical. It's pure sophistication in the guise of an earth-toned Pop-Tart.

Rye & Coffee Hand Pies

Makes 8 hand pies |

For the Hand Pies:

1 recipe Galette Dough (single crust, rye variation) (page 232)

½ jar Prune & Meyer Lemon Butter (page 145)

Line a cookie sheet with parchment paper.

Roll out the dough into a 16-inch square. Trim the edges and cut it into 16 squares. Place a scant tablespoon of the prune butter in the center of eight squares, spreading it out a little to leave a ¾-inch border all around. Brush the edges of these squares with cool water, then place an unadorned square on top. Seal the edges by pressing them with a fork. Use the fork to prick a few holes in the center of each parcel.

Place the hand pies on the prepared sheet and freeze for 1 hour. (Or freeze for up to 2 months, wrapped in plastic or sealed in an airtight container once frozen and then bake from frozen.)

Preheat the oven to 350°F (175°C). Line a cookie sheet with parchment paper.

Place the hand pies at least 1 inch apart on the prepared sheet and bake for 20 to 25 minutes, or until well browned on the bottom. Remove from the oven and let cool completely on the pan on a wire rack.

For the Glaze:

125 g (1 cup) icing sugar

1½ tsp instant coffee granules

45–90 mL (3–6 Tbsp) heavy cream

Ground coffee, to garnish (optional)

NOTE: *Can sub Bleu Matin Jam (page 179) or store-bought prune butter.*

To make the glaze, place the icing sugar in a medium bowl. In a measuring cup, dissolve the instant coffee in 45 mL (3 tablespoons) of heavy cream and then whisk it into the icing sugar until a spreadable consistency is achieved. You may need to add up to 45 mL (3 tablespoons) of cream, 1 tablespoon at a time.

Use a mini offset spatula or a knife to spread the glaze on the hand pies. Sprinkle with ground coffee, if using. Let the glaze set. These are best enjoyed the day they are made, but they are also pretty darn good the next day. (Keep them in an airtight container at room temperature overnight.)

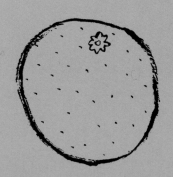

This jam is a great solution for those times when you come home from the farmers' market with a half pint of every berry you couldn't resist buying but aren't sure what to do with them. I came up with this recipe when I moved to a house with my first real honest-to-god garden in the ground and started planting the berries I'd always dreamed of growing: black and golden raspberries, black currants, and jostaberries. The trouble is, most berries take a few years to get established, so I only had a handful of each the first few years. On their own, each bush's harvest was just a snack, but together they made a jam. This recipe also works very well with frozen fruit. If you buy an extra half pint of berries every time you go to the market, throw them in the freezer and come November, when you're facing the true onset of winter, you can make what tastes like British summer pudding, a mixture of juicy sweetened berries encased in soft white bread.

Summer Pudding Jam

Makes five 250 mL (8 oz) jars

1.2 kg (about 8 cups) washed and hulled or stemmed mixed berries (see note)

675 g (3¼ cups + 2 Tbsp) sugar

60 mL (¼ cup) lemon juice

NOTE: *I leave most of the berries whole, but if the strawberries are large, I smoosh them by hand once they're macerated.*

In a large bowl, combine all of the ingredients and macerate for at least 15 minutes, or up to 1 week, covered, in the refrigerator.

Prepare the jars (see page 20).

Transfer the mixture to a pot or preserving pan. Heat on medium-high and bring to a hard boil, stirring frequently.

When the setting point is reached (see page 23), remove from the heat and pour into the prepared jars to within ¼ to ⅛ inch of the rim. Wipe the rims if necessary, seal, and invert for 1 to 2 minutes. Flip right side up and let the jam sit, undisturbed, for 24 hours.

I'd been searching for a good peanut butter cookie recipe for ages, as I found they were all either flabby or dry, too wet or too sandy. Then I made the recipe from Tara O'Brady's beautiful cookbook, *Seven Spoons*, and finally found a winner. I tweaked the proportions and swapped in some kamut flour, whose golden hue amplifies the peanut's color, and turned them into my own personal peanut butter cookie. That said, most sweet, rich cookies could use a dose of acidity for balance—enter berry jam. These are the most perfect peanut butter cookies I have ever met.

Kamut Peanut Butter Sandwich Cookies

Makes 10 sandwich cookies

200 g (¾ cup) natural smooth peanut butter

115 g (½ cup) unsalted butter, softened

140 g (⅔ cup) light brown sugar

75 g (¼ cup + 2 Tbsp) sugar

1 Tbsp honey

1 egg

1 tsp vanilla extract

70 g (½ cup) all-purpose flour

80 g (⅔ cup) kamut flour

¾ tsp baking soda

½ tsp salt

½ jar Summer Pudding Jam (page 154)

Preheat the oven to 350°F (175°C). Line two cookie sheets with parchment paper.

In a stand mixer fitted with the paddle attachment, cream the peanut butter, butter, both sugars, and honey on medium speed until smooth and well blended, but not light and fluffy. Beat in the egg, followed by the vanilla. With the mixer running on low speed, gently mix in both flours, the baking soda, and salt until homogeneous.

Use a 1-ounce cookie scoop or scoop 2 tablespoons to portion the dough, 2 inches apart, onto the prepared cookie sheets. (You should have 20 evenly sized pieces of dough.) Flatten the cookies a little with your moistened palm. (At this point you can freeze the unbaked dough and simply bake as needed from frozen, which may take a few minutes longer.)

NOTE: *Can sub Raspberry Lambic Jam (page 91), Bleu Matin Jam (page 179), or a good-quality store-bought blackberry jam.*

Bake for about 15 minutes, until golden brown around the edges. Take the cookies out of the oven and give the pan a nice slam on the countertop to deflate the cookies a little to make them less cakey. Let cool completely on the pans on wire racks. The cookies will keep in an airtight container at room temperature for up to 4 days before you've sandwiched them.

To serve, pair the cookies up, and spread about 2 teaspoons of jam onto the bottom of one and sandwich gently with its partner. Repeat. These will keep in an airtight container at room temperature for 2 days, although they'll be a little softer on the second day.

These are sturdy enough for a lunch box but elegant enough to serve as a petit four dusted with a little powdered sugar. How many squares can you say that about?

Pistachio Blondies

Makes 25 squares |

80 g (½ cup) pistachios, plus a small handful for topping

140 g (1 cup) all-purpose flour

1 tsp salt

½ tsp baking powder

¼ tsp baking soda

145 g (10 Tbsp) Brown Butter (page 228)

275 g (1¼ cups) brown sugar

1 egg

1 egg yolk

1 tsp vanilla extract

¾ tsp almond or pistachio extract

½ jar Summer Pudding Jam (page 154)

NOTE: *Can sub Raspberry Lambic Jam (page 91), Black Raspberry Jam (page 52), Tutti Frutti Jam (page 185), or any good-quality store-bought berry jam.*

Recipe pictured on page 158

Preheat the oven to 350°F (175°C). Grease an 8-inch square pan with butter or nonstick spray and line with parchment paper.

Grind the pistachios in a food processor fitted with the steel blade until very fine. (Or chop them by hand until they are as fine as is humanly possible.) Transfer to a small bowl and whisk together with the flour, salt, baking powder, and baking soda.

Melt the brown butter in a small saucepan over medium heat, then transfer to a medium mixing bowl. Whisk in the sugar until well blended, followed by the egg and yolk, and then the extracts. Fold in the flour mixture.

Transfer to the prepared pan, smoothing out the top with a mini offset spatula, then dollop teaspoons of jam all over the surface. Roughly chop a small handful of pistachios and scatter over top.

Bake for about 40 minutes, until deep golden brown and set in the middle. Let cool completely in the pan on a wire rack before cutting into squares.

The blondies will keep in an airtight container at room temperature for at least 4 days.

Pistachio Blondies (page 157)

This jam makes me think of picnics in the English countryside, Pimm's cups, and croquet. It's a good case study for anyone creating their own flavors. It follows the same principles as the Strawberry Margarita Jam from my first book, but couldn't be more different!

Rhubarb Lemonade Jam with Elderflower

Makes five 250 mL (8 oz) jars

200 g (1½ large) lemons

500 mL (2 cups) water

1 kg (7 cups) chopped rhubarb

867 g (4⅓ cups) sugar

1½ Tbsp elderflower liqueur
    (such as St-Germain) (see note)

———————

NOTE: *If you're not an imbiber, you can substitute nonalcoholic elderflower cordial for the liqueur (hint: Ikea makes a good one).*

———————

Quarter the lemons lengthwise and slice them thinly into little triangles, keeping the peels on but discarding any seeds. Place them in a medium pot with the water, cover, and soak overnight.

The next day remove the cover and bring the lemons and water to a boil. Turn down the heat and simmer until the peels are tender and most of the water has evaporated, about 40 minutes. In the meantime, in a large bowl, mix the rhubarb with the sugar and macerate at room temperature until the lemons are ready.

Prepare the jars (see page 20).

When the lemons are ready, add them to the rhubarb-sugar mixture. Transfer to a wide, heavy-bottomed pan and bring to a boil over medium-high heat. Cook at a rolling boil, stirring frequently, until the froth subsides and the bubbles become regular and sputter violently.

When the setting point has been reached (see page 23), remove from the heat and add the elderflower liqueur. Pour into the prepared jars to within ¼ to ⅛ inch of the rim. Wipe the rims if necessary, seal, and invert for 1 to 2 minutes. Flip right side up and let the jam sit, undisturbed, for 24 hours.

Rhubarb Lemonade Jam with Elderflower (page 159) and Victoria Sandwich (pictured right)

I have a serious aversion to airplane food, so I try to never fly without bringing my own meal. I've been lucky enough to visit Ireland and England over the past few years, and I became a little obsessed with pre-airport M&S Food Hall visits for provisions. I always got a slice of the Victoria sandwich—a rectangular cross-section of cake filled with sweet strawberry jam and buttercream and dusted with icing sugar. It's always sad to leave one of my favorite places, where so many of the baked goods I love are so readily available.

So I made a little more sophisticated—but still very much British—version with rhubarb, lemon, and elderflower. You might notice that this is similar to the Victoria sponge from *The Great British Bake Off*. If you like, bake it in two 8-inch round pans instead of a loaf pan, as I do here. You can also use whipped cream instead of icing, but do note that this makes it much harder to put a slice in your purse to take on the plane.

Victoria Sandwich

Makes one (two-layer) 5- x 9-inch cake |

For the Cake:

210 g (1½ cups) all-purpose flour

30 g (3 Tbsp) tapioca starch

2 tsp baking powder

½ tsp salt

230 g (1 cup) unsalted butter, softened

175 g (¾ cup + 2 Tbsp) sugar

4 large eggs, at room temperature

2 tsp vanilla extract

60–90 mL (4–6 Tbsp) whole milk

Preheat the oven to 350°F (175°C). Grease a 5- x 9-inch loaf pan with butter or nonstick spray and line with parchment paper.

In a small bowl, whisk together the flour, tapioca starch, baking powder, and salt.

In a stand mixer fitted with the paddle attachment, cream the butter and sugar on medium speed until light and fluffy. Add the eggs one by one, following each addition with a spoonful of the flour mixture to prevent curdling. Once all the eggs are in, scrape down the sides of the bowl, then add the vanilla. Add the remaining flour mixture and mix on low speed until

For the Filling:

77 g (⅓ cup) unsalted butter, softened

63 g (½ cup) icing sugar

Zest of ½ lemon

1½ tsp elderflower liqueur (such as St-Germain)

½ jar Rhubarb Lemonade Jam with Elderflower (page 159)

To Finish:

Icing sugar

Fresh elderflowers and/or candied lemon slices (optional)

NOTE: *Can sub Raspberry Lambic Jam (page 91), Strawberry & Passion Fruit Jam (page 84), or a good-quality store-bought rhubarb and/or strawberry jam.*

---

combined. Mix in the milk, 1 tablespoon at a time, until the mixture is thinned out enough to drop off the spatula with a satisfying plonk when lifted.

Scrape the batter evenly into the prepared pan, and bake for about 1 hour, until golden brown and an instant read thermometer inserted into the center of the cake reads 210°F (99°C) or a toothpick inserted in the center comes out with just one or two moist crumbs attached.

Let the cake cool in the pan on a wire rack for 20 minutes before removing from the pan and letting cool completely on the rack. When it's cool, use a serrated knife to slice the cake into two layers.

To make the filling, in a stand mixer fitted with the paddle attachment, cream the butter, icing sugar, lemon zest, and liqueur on medium-high speed until light and fluffy.

Using an offset spatula, spread the icing evenly over the bottom layer of the cake, followed by the jam. Top with the other layer, pressing down gently so they adhere. Dust with icing sugar to finish, if desired. If you can rustle up some fresh elderflowers and/or candied lemons to decorate the top, that would be nice, too! This is best the day it's made, but it will keep at room temperature, well wrapped, for 5 days (hello, transatlantic flight!).

I realize that many people will dissent here, but I've never been that fond of lemon desserts. I can't explain it. I love both acid and citrus, but when it comes to dessert I always opt for another fruit. That said, I find eating one of these little cakes is pure bliss. Best served warm, it's both cakey and pudding-y (as the name would suggest)—two delights in concert. It's comforting, but also quite chic, especially when topped with crème fraîche and extra jam. And while there's something very special about getting your own personal cake, if you don't have ramekins or wide-mouth jars handy you can use a large (2-quart) oval baking dish; you'll just need to bake it 15 minutes or so longer.

Lemon Pudding Cakes

Serves 6 |

3 large eggs, separated

150 g (¾ cup) sugar, divided

⅓ jar Rhubarb Lemonade Jam with Elderflower (page 159)

80 mL (⅓ cup) lemon juice

Zest of 1 lemon

47 g (⅓ cup) all-purpose flour

½ tsp salt

220 mL (¾ cup + 2 Tbsp) whole milk

58 g (¼ cup) butter, melted, cooled

1 Tbsp elderflower liqueur (such as St-Germain) (optional)

Crème fraîche, to serve (optional)

Preheat the oven to 350°F (175°C). Grease six 6-ounce ramekins and place them in a 9- x 13-inch baking pan.

Bring a kettle full of water to a boil.

In a medium bowl, whisk together the egg yolks and 100 grams (½ cup) of the sugar. Whisk in the jam, lemon juice, and zest, followed by the flour and salt. Finally, whisk in the milk, butter, and liqueur, if using.

In a stand mixer fitted with the whisk attachment, whip the egg whites on medium-high speed until they begin to form soft peaks. With the mixer running, gradually add the remaining 50 grams (¼ cup) of sugar and continue to whip until glossy and firm.

NOTE: *Can sub Rhume Rx Jelly (page 205) (sub whisky for the elderflower liqueur), A Different Seville Marmalade (page 70) (sub Seville orange juice for the lemon juice), or a good-quality store-bought lemon marmalade.*

Gently fold the egg whites into the batter and divide between the ramekins. Place the pan in the oven and carefully pour in boiling water (make sure you don't splash any into the ramekins) until it reaches a little over halfway up the sides of the ramekins.

Bake for about 35 minutes, until golden brown. Remove the pan from the oven and carefully remove the ramekins to a wire rack to cool slightly. Serve posthaste with crème fraîche and extra jam, if you like. Leftovers can be refrigerated, covered, for up to 3 days.

When I sold this jam it had a very loyal following. It was the result of a collaboration between Preservation Society and Dillon's Distillers, a small-batch distillery in Niagara. We settled on combining sour cherries with the classic Negroni cocktail, which is a mixture of gin, sweet red vermouth, and Campari. We used their gin, vermouth, and Orangecello, but you can of course use any brand of gin, sweet vermouth, and bitter aperitivo. Sour cherries can be challenging to make into jam, as they have very little pectin. While for the most part I make jams without pectin, for this I used a little low-sugar pectin to get a soft set, once a lot of the water had cooked off and the jam had the concentrated cherry flavor I was looking for. That said, you don't need to use it if you prefer not to. Just be aware that you will end up with fewer jars, as you'll have to cook off more moisture to thicken the mixture.

Cherry Negroni Jam

Makes four to five 250 mL (8 oz) jars

1 kg (6½ cups) pitted sour cherries

575 g (2¾ cups + 2 Tbsp) sugar

45 mL (3 Tbsp) lemon juice

1 (49 g) package no-sugar-needed pectin

½ oz gin

½ oz sweet vermouth

½ oz Campari or Dillon's Orangecello

In a large bowl or container, combine the sour cherries, sugar, and lemon juice and let macerate for at least 15 minutes, or up to 1 week, covered, in the refrigerator.

Prepare the jars (see page 20).

Transfer the mixture to a pot or preserving pan and heat on medium-high, stirring occasionally. When the mixture comes to a boil, ladle out a few cups and carefully purée them (hot liquids can be volatile) in a blender to add body to the jam, since the cherries don't really break down. Return the blended cherries to the pan and boil hard again, stirring frequently.

When the jam has reduced and thickened and is looking jammy, slowly add the pectin, stirring constantly. Let the jam cook for a few more minutes until the setting point is reached (see page 23). Remove from the heat and add all the liquor, stirring to combine. Pour into the prepared jars to within ¼ to ⅛ inch of the rim. Remove any air bubbles, wipe the rims if necessary, seal, and invert for 1 to 2 minutes. Flip right side up and let the jam sit, undisturbed, for 24 hours.

Recipe pictured on page 169

The Empire cookie goes by many names—Belgian biscuit, biscuit bun, German biscuit, double biscuit—and is apparently related to the Linzertorte, which I suppose it must be, in as much as any jam-filled pastry is. I do not think, however, that it has ever been quite this good. The Cherry Negroni Jam and the gin work perfectly here, but you could technically sub in any jam and flavor the glaze to match, creating your own perfect Empire cookie. Again, though, I'm not sure this version can be improved upon!

Empire Cookies with Gin Glaze

Makes 24 sandwich cookies |

For the Cookies:

230 g (1 cup) unsalted butter, softened

150 g (¾ cup) sugar

1 tsp vanilla extract

325 g (2⅓ cups) all-purpose flour

¼ tsp salt

In a stand mixer fitted with the paddle attachment, cream the butter and sugar on medium speed until light and fluffy. Add the vanilla and mix to combine. Add the flour and salt, and mix on low speed until a dough forms. Pat into a disk, wrap in plastic, and refrigerate until firm enough to roll, between 30 minutes and 1 hour. (Or you can make the dough up to 1 week in advance and refrigerate or freeze it. Bring it to room temperature before proceeding.)

Preheat the oven to 350°F (175°C). Line three cookie sheets with parchment paper.

On a floured surface, roll out the dough to ⅛ inch thick. Cut into 48 rounds using a 2-inch fluted cutter. (You may need to gather the scraps and roll again to get the 48.)

Bake for 10 to 12 minutes, until firm and just golden around the edges. Let cool completely on the pan on a wire rack.

To Finish:

⅓ jar Cherry Negroni Jam (page 165), puréed or finely chopped

94 g (¾ cup) icing sugar

3 Tbsp gin

12 candied cherries (Amarena, cocktail, or maraschino), drained and halved

---

NOTE: *Can sub Rhubarb & Amarena Cherry Jam (page 78) (use Amarena syrup for glaze), Rhubarb Lemonade Jam with Elderflower (page 159) (use elderflower liqueur for glaze), or good-quality store-bought sour cherry jam.*

To finish the cookies, using a mini offset spatula, spread about ½ teaspoon of jam onto the bottom of half the cookies.

In a small bowl, whisk the icing sugar with the gin until smooth. Dip the tops of the remaining cookies into the glaze, shaking off any excess, and place each one on top of a jam-covered cookie. Place half a cherry in the center of each. Let the glaze set for about 30 minutes before serving or storing between sheets of wax paper. The sandwiched cookies will keep at room temperature in an airtight container for 5 days.

Cherry Negroni Jam (page 165)

My good friend Laurel Wypkema is not only the inspiration for one of my favorite jams in this book (Tutti Frutti, page 185), she is also the creator of this extremely delicious ice cream and was generous enough to share the recipe.

Laurel notes that this ice cream is just as delicious with vanilla in place of the zest and bitters. You can either use the seeds and pod of half a vanilla bean simmered in the milk (remove the pod before adding the milk to the yolks), or 1 teaspoon of good-quality vanilla extract once your custard is cooled. (You'll need an ice cream maker for this.)

Cherry Negroni Jam Swirl Ice Cream

Makes about 1½ pints

75 g (¼ cup + 2 Tbsp) sugar

⅛ tsp guar gum (optional) (see note)

200 mL (¾ cup + 1 Tbsp) heavy cream

100 mL (⅓ cup + 1 Tbsp) whole milk

60 g (3) egg yolks

Zest of ½ orange

Pinch of salt

1 tsp orange bitters

⅓ jar Cherry Negroni Jam, chilled (page 165)

In a bowl, whisk the sugar thoroughly with the guar gum, if using.

Prepare an ice bath by half-filling a large mixing bowl with very cold water and lots of ice. Refrigerate until needed.

Set a fine mesh strainer atop a medium heatproof bowl.

In a heavy-bottomed saucepan over medium heat, bring the cream and milk to a simmer and then immediately remove from the heat. In a medium bowl, add the egg yolks to the sugar and whisk well. Whisking constantly, pour the hot cream into the yolks in a steady stream. Return this mixture to the pan, add the zest and a pinch of salt, and continue cooking on low heat, stirring constantly with a heatproof spatula. Cook the egg yolk and thicken the custard until it reaches 180°F (82°C), or the custard coats the back of a spoon and is sturdy enough to hold its shape when you draw your finger across the back of the spoon. Be careful not to overcook it.

Guar gum is a stabilizer made from the seeds of the guar plant, and can be found in health food stores. It helps improve the texture of the finished ice cream by adding to its viscosity and keeping it from developing ice crystals. You can omit the guar gum entirely if you prefer (especially since it will be impossible and/or ridiculous to buy less than a single gram of it), or substitute 1 teaspoon of cornstarch whisked into 1 tablespoon of milk and added to the simmering milk/cream/sugar about a minute before you remove it from the heat. Can sub Tutti Frutti Jam (page 185), Purple Rain Jam (page 192, vanilla variation), or a good-quality store-bought cherry jam.

Remove the custard from the heat and pour it through the strainer into the bowl. Nestle the bowl into the ice bath, stirring constantly to cool the custard as quickly as possible. Once cooled to room temperature, cover with plastic wrap directly on the surface of the custard to prevent a skin from forming and refrigerate until very cold, ideally overnight.

Just before churning, put the container in which you'll store your finished ice cream into the freezer. Stir the bitters into the custard, then churn according to the ice cream maker manufacturer's instructions. Be sure to stop churning once your ice cream is the consistency of soft serve. Alternate layers of ice cream and jam into your pre-frozen container, then gently swirl a spoon through to better incorporate the jam. Cover tightly and place in the coldest part of your freezer and freeze for at least 6 hours before serving. The ice cream will keep for 1 month in the freezer.

I've always liked the transmogrification of classic desserts into sweet things of a different nature. If I see a chocolate bonbon version of Bananas Foster or a birthday cake–flavored gum, I have to buy it, often in spite of my better judgment. This is one stellar example, though—and probably the most universally adored jam at my fruit-canning workshops.

It is also an unusual instance in which frozen fruit might actually produce a superior result. I have made this using fresh sour cherries picked in the alleys of Montreal as well as with frozen French griottes, and I preferred the latter. This allows you to make this excellent jam even in the deep freeze of winter, and to save your summer sour cherries for other noble pursuits.

Black Forest Jam

Makes four 250 mL (8 oz) jars

1.2 kg (7¾ cups) pitted sour cherries

800 g (4 cups) sugar

1 vanilla bean, split and scraped

125 mL (½ cup) crabapple juice (page 63) (optional)

60 mL (¼ cup) lemon juice

24 g (3 Tbsp) cocoa nibs

45 mL (3 Tbsp) kirsch or cherry brandy

In a pot or preserving pan, combine the cherries, sugar, vanilla bean, crabapple juice, if using, and lemon juice. Let macerate, uncovered, for at least 15 minutes, or up to 1 week, in the refrigerator.

Prepare the jars (see page 20).

Heat on medium-high, stirring occasionally, and stir in the cocoa nibs once the mixture comes to a boil.

Continue to boil hard, stirring frequently. When the setting point is reached (see page 23), remove from the heat. Remove the vanilla bean and add the kirsch. Pour into the prepared jars to within ¼ to ⅛ inch of the rim. Remove any air bubbles, wipe the rims if necessary, seal, and invert for 1 to 2 minutes. Flip right side up and let the jam sit, undisturbed, for 24 hours.

The strange truth about me is that I'm not really that into chocolate desserts, and I'm often very against combining chocolate with fruit. Cherries, however, are the exception. It's also a little funny to make a jam based on a cake flavor and then turn it back into a cake, but the more I think about it, the better an idea it seems—like a Black Forest ouroboros! Whatever the case, this is a real crowd-pleaser, and if you use tapioca starch instead of flour, it will even please the gluten-free crowd.

Black Forest Torte

Makes one 9-inch cake |

For the Cake:

260 g (9 oz) dark chocolate

130 g (½ cup + 1 Tbsp) unsalted butter, cubed

6 large eggs, separated

½ jar Black Forest Jam (page 172)

2 Tbsp tapioca starch or all-purpose flour

¼ tsp salt

75 g (¼ cup + 2 Tbsp) sugar

Preheat the oven to 350°F (175°C). Grease an 8½-inch springform pan with butter or nonstick spray and line with parchment paper.

To make the cake, in a large heatproof bowl set over a pot of simmering water, or in the microwave in 20- to 30-second bursts, melt the chocolate and butter together. Let cool for a few minutes before whisking in the egg yolks, followed by the jam, tapioca starch or all-purpose flour, and salt.

In a stand mixer fitted with the whisk attachment, whip the egg whites on medium-high speed until soft peaks form. With the mixer running, gradually add the sugar. Continue to whisk until firm peaks form.

Mix about one-third of the egg whites into the chocolate mixture to lighten it, then gently fold in the remaining egg whites. Transfer to the prepared baking pan.

For the Topping:

375 mL (1½ cups) heavy cream

1–2 Tbsp kirsch

1 tsp vanilla paste

½ jar Black Forest Jam (page 172)

1 cherry (optional)

NOTE: *Can sub a good-quality store-bought cherry jam.*

Bake for 30 minutes, until just set. Cool completely in the pan on a wire rack. Remove from the pan once you're ready to make the topping.

To make the topping, in a stand mixer fitted with the whisk attachment, whip the cream with the kirsch and vanilla paste on medium-high speed to medium peaks. Gently swirl in the jam, then spread it all over the top of the cake, swirling it into artful peaks. Finish with a single cherry, if you like. This cake is best served the day it is made, but any leftovers will keep in the refrigerator, covered, for 2 to 3 days.

You might know these by the brand names Mallomars, Whippets, or Viva Puffs. They're chocolate-covered marshmallow cookies. These particular ones combine the nostalgia of childhood with sophisticated flavors, one of my favorite baking moves.

Are these a project? Yes, indubitably. But if you have a free afternoon, you will make a lot of people very happy with these and hone your marshmallow-making skills to boot.

Black Forest Puffs

Makes about 34 cookies |

For the Cookie Base:

225 g (1½ cups + 2 Tbsp) all-purpose flour

55 g (½ cup) cocoa powder

¼ tsp salt

215 g (¾ cup + 3 Tbsp) unsalted butter, softened

150 g (¾ cup) sugar

1 large egg, at room temperature

1 tsp vanilla extract

¾ jar Black Forest Jam (page 172)

NOTE: *Can sub Raspberry Lambic Jam (page 91) or good-quality store-bought cherry jam.*

To make the cookie base, sift together the flour, cocoa powder, and salt. In a stand mixer fitted with the paddle attachment, cream the butter and sugar on medium speed until light and fluffy. Add the egg and vanilla, and mix to combine. Add the flour mixture and mix on low speed until a dough forms. Pat into a disk, wrap in plastic, and refrigerate until firm enough to roll, between 30 minutes and 1 hour. (Or you can make the dough up to 1 week in advance and refrigerate or freeze it. Just let it come to cool room temperature before proceeding.)

Preheat the oven to 350°F (175°C). Line three cookie sheets with parchment paper.

On a floured surface, roll out the dough to ¼ inch thick. Cut it into 34 rounds, or as many as you can, using a 2½-inch plain cutter. You may need to gather the scraps and roll again. Bake for 10 to 12 minutes, until firm and just beginning to darken around the edges. Let cool completely on the pans on a wire rack.

For the Marshmallow:

30 g (15 sheets) gelatin

400 g (2 cups) sugar

155 g (½ cup.) glucose or light corn syrup

125 mL (½ cup) water

60 g (2) egg whites

¼ tsp salt

1 Tbsp kirsch

1 Tbsp vanilla paste

To Finish:

172 g (6 oz) dark chocolate

1 Tbsp coconut oil

Cocoa nibs, for sprinkling (optional)

Transfer the cookies to a wire rack set over a rimmed baking sheet. Top each one with a scant teaspoon of jam.

To make the marshmallow, in a deep measuring cup, soak the gelatin in cold water. Once it's hydrated, drain and reserve.

In a small pot on medium-high heat, combine the sugar, glucose, and water and bring to a boil.

In the meantime, in a stand mixer fitted with the whisk attachment, whip the egg whites with the salt on medium-high speed until foamy and soft peaks form.

When the sugar mixture reaches 240°F (116°C) on an instant read thermometer, immediately remove from the heat and stir in the drained gelatin to dissolve. With the mixer running on medium speed, slowly pour the hot syrup into the egg whites, staying close to the side of the bowl to prevent the whisk from catching the syrup and sending it off in all directions. When the syrup has been added, turn the mixer up to high speed and whip the mixture until it is almost cool. Add the kirsch and vanilla, mixing to combine.

Transfer the marshmallow to a pastry bag fitted with a large plain no. 6 tip (5 or 7 would do too). Pipe a little test to make sure it holds its shape. If not, return to the mixer and continue to whip.

Pipe kiss-like blobs onto the cookies, covering the jam entirely. Leave a small border around the edge of the cookies so the marshmallow doesn't overflow. Leave to set at room temperature for a few hours, or up to overnight at room temperature.

To finish, melt the chocolate with the coconut oil in a heatproof bowl set over a pot of simmering water, or in the microwave in 20- to 30-second bursts. You can either dip the cookies into the chocolate, trying to get all the marshmallow covered and shaking to remove any excess, or set them on a wire rack set inside a rimmed baking sheet and ladle the chocolate over top. Sprinkle with a few cocoa nibs, if you like.

Let the chocolate set before serving (throw them into the refrigerator to speed this up if you like). These will keep at room temperature in an airtight container for up to 3 days.

Originally, I was going to call this blueberry jam Blue Monday after the song by New Order, but turns out it's also the name for what is reputedly the most depressing day of the year. Seemed a little dark for jam. Instead I went with Bleu Matin, French for "blue morning." If you really slur it sounds a bit like "bon matin" (good morning). I use a mixture of wild and cultivated blueberries. The wild have more flavor, but I like the way the cultivated ones break down and make a smooth base. That said, you can use all of one or the other and still get great results.

Bleu Matin Jam

Makes four 250 mL (8 oz) jars

1.5 kg (12 cups) washed and stemmed blueberries

700 g (3½ cups) sugar

75 mL (5 Tbsp) lemon juice

1½ Tbsp coffee beans

In a large bowl, combine the blueberries, sugar, and lemon juice, and let macerate for at least 15 minutes, or up to 1 week, covered, in the refrigerator.

Prepare the jars (see page 20).

Transfer the mixture to a pot or preserving pan. Put the coffee beans in a large tea ball or tie them up in a piece of cheesecloth and add to the pot. Heat on medium, stirring often, until the blueberries begin to give up some juice and the sugar starts to dissolve. Ladle out about one-third of the mixture into a blender and purée (with caution—it's hot!), before returning to the pot. Increase the heat to medium-high and bring to a hard boil, stirring frequently.

When the setting point is reached (see page 23), remove from the heat and discard the coffee beans.

Ladle into the prepared jars to within ¼ to ⅛ inch of the rim. Remove any air bubbles, wipe the rims if necessary, seal, and invert for 1 to 2 minutes. Flip right side up and let the jam sit, undisturbed, for 24 hours.

Blueberries, coffee, and maple sound like the ingredients for a scrumptious breakfast, but here they take a more sophisticated turn in the form of a dramatic layer cake. If you love baking but don't yet own any 6-inch cake pans, consider investing. I love layer cakes, but I find an 8- or 9-inch cake almost impossible to finish, even with a lot of people to help.

Breakfast Layer Cake

Makes one (four-layer) 6-inch cake |

For the Cake:

180 g (1⅓ cups) all-purpose flour

¾ tsp baking powder

½ tsp baking soda

½ tsp salt

115 g (½ cup) unsalted butter, softened

200 g (1 cup) sugar

2 large eggs, at room temperature

1 tsp vanilla extract

165 mL (⅔ cup) buttermilk,
    at room temperature

NOTE: *Can sub a good-quality store-bought blueberry jam.*

To make the cake, preheat the oven to 350°F (175°C). Grease two 6-inch cake pans with butter or nonstick spray and line the bottoms with parchment paper.

In a medium bowl, whisk together the flour, baking powder, baking soda, and salt.

In a stand mixer fitted with the paddle attachment, cream the butter with the sugar on medium-high speed until pale and fluffy. Add the eggs one at a time, beating well after each addition. Add the vanilla.

With the mixer running on low speed, add one-third of the flour mixture, alternating with half the buttermilk, until everything is incorporated.

Divide the batter evenly between the two pans, and bake for about 25 minutes, until a toothpick inserted into the center of each cake comes out with just a few moist crumbs attached.

Let cool in the pans on a wire rack for 15 minutes. Remove from the pans, place directly on the wire racks, and let cool entirely. At this point the cakes can be wrapped in plastic wrap and refrigerated for up to 1 day, or frozen for up to 2 months.

For the Coffee Syrup:

50 g (¼ cup) sugar

90 mL (¼ cup + 2 Tbsp) hot strong coffee

1 tsp vanilla extract

For the Maple Buttercream:

90 g (3) egg whites

Pinch of salt

250 mL (1 cup) maple syrup

290 g (1¼ cups) unsalted butter, softened

To Finish:

1 jar Bleu Matin Jam (page 179)

Ground coffee and/or chocolate-covered espresso beans

Bachelor's button edible flowers (optional)

To make the coffee syrup, in a medium bowl, whisk the sugar into the hot coffee until dissolved. Let cool. Stir in the vanilla and set aside.

To make the maple buttercream, put the egg whites and a pinch of salt in a stand mixer fitted with the whisk attachment. Start to beat them on medium-low speed. Meanwhile, in a small pot on medium-high heat, heat the maple syrup until it reaches 238°F (114°C) on an instant read thermometer. Increase the mixer speed to medium when the syrup is close to being ready. Once the syrup has reached the target temperature, immediately take it off the heat and slowly and carefully pour it into the egg whites while they're whipping, trying to avoid hitting the whisk so it doesn't splatter. Once all the syrup has been added, turn the mixer speed up to high and let it beat until the mixture is voluminous and cool to the touch, about 5 to 10 minutes. Turn the mixer back down to medium speed and begin to add the butter, tablespoon by tablespoon. If the mixture starts to look broken or curdled, don't despair. Just turn the mixer up to high speed and whip it for a few minutes. It should all come back together, smooth and glossy.

To assemble the cake, use a long serrated knife to cut both cakes in half horizontally so that you have four layers. Save the nicest for the top. Affix the first layer to a cake board or stand with a little buttercream, then use a pastry brush to cover the surface of the cake with the coffee syrup. Next, spread one-third of the jam to within ½ inch of the edge of the cake. Use a mini offset spatula to spread about ⅓ cup of the buttercream on top of the jam, then top with the next layer, pressing down slightly. Repeat with the second and third layers, and then place the final cake layer, cut side down, on top. Brush it with syrup and spread a very thin layer of the maple buttercream all over the cake. This is called the crumb coat and it will make it much easier to ice the cake. Place the cake in the refrigerator for 15 minutes to let the buttercream harden.

To finish the cake, frost it with the rest of the buttercream. Decorate the top with ground coffee and/or chocolate-covered espresso beans and edible flowers, if using.

Serve at once, or refrigerate it overnight and bring it to room temperature before serving. Any leftovers will keep, covered, in the refrigerator for up to 4 days.

These are magical in that even people who dislike meringues enjoy them. Although I'm personally a meringue lover, I can see how one might be averse to their plain sugar flavor and sometimes chalky texture. I like eating these best the day they're made, when they still have that crunchy, chalky exterior and are slightly squishy inside, but everyone else seems to love them the next day when the outside is crumbly and yielding. You can eat them as is or sandwich them with more jam or whipped cream (or both) for a real treat.

Coffee-Dusted Meringues

Makes fifteen 2-inch meringues |

90 g (3) egg whites, at room temperature

150 g (¾ cup) sugar

1 vanilla bean, split and scraped

60 mL (¼ cup) Bleu Matin Jam (page 179)

Ground espresso, for sprinkling (optional)

Freeze-dried blueberries, for sprinkling (optional)

Preheat the oven to 200°F (93°C). Line a large cookie sheet with parchment paper.

To make the meringue, in the bowl of a stand mixer set over a pot of simmering water (making sure the bowl doesn't touch the water), whisk together (by hand) the egg whites and sugar. Heat, whisking constantly, until the mixture is warm to the touch.

Transfer the bowl back to the stand mixer, fitted with the whisk attachment. Beat on high speed until the mixture is cool and holds stiff peaks. Add the vanilla seeds and mix on medium speed a few seconds to incorporate. Transfer about ½ cup of the meringue to a small bowl. Add the jam to the bowl and fold it in until well incorporated. Fold this mixture back into the plain meringue, being careful not to overmix—we want a marbled effect!

NOTE: *Can sub Coffee, Date, & Pear Jam (page 198) (top with ground espresso), Apricot & Cocoa Nib Jam (page 103) (top with cocoa nibs), or a good-quality store-bought blueberry jam.*

Using a 2-ounce ice cream scoop, or even just a spoon, scoop out roughly 2-inch demi-spheres onto the prepared cookie sheet. Sprinkle with espresso powder, if using. Crush the blueberries between your fingers for a rough texture and sprinkle over top, if using.

Bake for 1½ to 2 hours, until the meringues are ever so slightly browned and sound hollow when tapped on the bottom. Turn off the oven, set the door ajar, and let the meringues cool inside. This will take an hour or two.

You can store these in an airtight container at room temperature for up to 3 days.

My friend Laurel runs a cool one-woman ice cream company called Foundry (see her recipe contribution on page 170). One year she was obsessed with making the ultimate tutti frutti ice cream and asked if I would candy all sorts of fruits to help her realize her dream. Unfortunately, I was moving at the time, so she went ahead and did it on her own. The idea stayed with me, though, and when I was settled in Toronto I made the ultimate tutti frutti jam in her honor. Because both Laurel and I go overboard at the farmers' market, I made this recipe very adaptable. You can make it with any combination of yellow, orange, and white summer fruits, as long as you make the weight and use some high-pectin fruits. The first time, I made it with white currants, yellow Rainier cherries, an apricot, yellow plums, and peaches. The second time, I used white peaches, fresh sea buckthorn, apricots, and yellow plums. Both versions were superlative.

Tutti Frutti Jam

Makes four 250 mL (8 oz) jars

1.25 kg (6½–8 cups) washed, pitted, and/or stemmed mixed stone fruit and berries, hued from white to cream to yellow to orange (see note)

625 g (3 cups + 2 Tbsp) sugar

75 mL (5 Tbsp) lemon juice

55 g (¼ cup) diced candied orange peel (preferably Seville)

½ vanilla bean, split and scraped

NOTE: *Leave berries whole, halve cherries, and slice or chop other stone fruit.*

In a large bowl, combine all of the ingredients and let macerate for at least 15 minutes, or up to 1 week, covered, in the refrigerator.

Prepare the jars (see page 20).

Transfer the mixture to a pot or preserving pan. Heat on medium-high and bring to a hard boil, stirring frequently.

When the setting point is reached (see page 23), remove from the heat and fish out the vanilla pod.

Ladle into the prepared jars to within ¼ to ⅛ inch of the rim. Wipe the rims if necessary, seal, and invert for 1 to 2 minutes. Flip right side up and let the jam sit, undisturbed, for 24 hours.

Recipe pictured on page 186

[front] Meringue Roll with Eau-de-Vie Cream (see right), *[back]* Tutti Frutti Jam (page 185)

Eau-de-vie is a clear fruit brandy with no added sugar. If you're not familiar with it, I highly recommend you track one down at your local liquor store. It's similar to schnapps, which will also work here, although slivovitz, a European plum brandy, might be easier to find. Also, while slivovitz works well here, ideally you want something more evocative of tutti frutti's color scheme, such as a Mirabelle plum or peach eau-de-vie. Whatever you choose, go for something that tastes like fruit but not sugar. The meringue and jam bring more than enough sweetness, although the cream is meant to temper that. Most people I've spoken to seem to prefer 2 tablespoons of eau-de-vie, so start with that—but I prefer 3 tablespoons in total, so add more if you like.

Meringue Roll with Eau-de-Vie Cream

Serves 6 to 8 |

For the Meringue:

180 g (6) egg whites, at room
temperature

350 g (1¾ cups) sugar

1½ tsp cornstarch

1½ tsp vanilla extract

1½ tsp white vinegar

Preheat the oven to 400°F (200°C). Grease a 10- x 15-inch jelly roll pan with butter or nonstick pan spray and line with parchment paper.

To make the meringue, in a stand mixer fitted with the whisk attachment, whip the egg whites on medium-high speed until soft peaks form. With the mixer running, gradually add the sugar, continuing to whip until stiff peaks form. Add the cornstarch, vanilla, and vinegar, then briefly mix to combine.

Using an offset spatula, spread the meringue evenly in the prepared pan.

Bake for 5 minutes, then turn down the oven to 350°F (175°C) and let the meringue bake for about 20 more minutes, just until it is starting to take on a little color and beginning to crack.

For the Filling:

375 mL (1½ cups) heavy cream

30–45 mL (2–3 Tbsp) eau-de-vie

1 jar Tutti Frutti Jam (page 185)

NOTE: *Can sub any good-quality store-bought mixed fruit jam (match the eau-de-vie accordingly!).*

Let cool completely on the pan on a wire rack. This will take about 1 hour.

Just before serving, make the filling. In a stand mixer fitted with the whisk attachment, whip the cream with the eau-de-vie on medium-high speed until firm peaks form.

Invert the meringue onto a piece of parchment a little larger than the pan and peel away the parchment from the bottom. Using a mini offset spatula, spread the jam over the meringue, leaving a 1-inch border along the long edge farthest from you. Do the same with the whipped cream, then carefully roll up the meringue toward the long edge with the border, using the parchment paper to help you. Slide it onto a serving platter. Use a serrated knife to cut generous slices.

The meringue roll will keep in an airtight container in the refrigerator for a few days. It will still taste delicious, but the texture will change as the meringue takes on moisture and loses its crunch, becoming more marshmallow-y. (Perhaps you prefer this and want to make it ahead?)

I have a very vivid memory of my grandmother serving Bakewell tarts to my cousin Tanis and me for a special high tea. There were little crustless cucumber sandwiches and too many sweets for the three of us to ever eat, which is to say it was a perfect afternoon. I think it might have been the first, and possibly last, time I had a Bakewell tart—they're a British specialty, and I haven't often come across them outside of the UK. Besides which, most commercial baked goods are made with a smattering of subpar jam. These, on the other hand, are sublime.

Bakewell Tarts

Makes 12 tarts |

For the Tarts:

1 recipe Sweet Tart Dough (page 230)

⅓ jar Tutti Frutti Jam (page 185)

½ recipe Frangipane (page 233)

For the Glaze:

63 g (½ cup) icing sugar

¼ tsp orange zest

¼ tsp vanilla paste

2–3 Tbsp heavy cream

Preheat the oven to 375°F (190°C). Grease 12 muffin cups with butter.

To make the tarts, roll out the sweet dough to ⅛ inch thick. Using a 4-inch plain round cutter, cut out 12 rounds. You may need to gather the scraps and roll again. Fit the dough rounds into the bottom and up the sides of each muffin cup. Prick the bottom and sides with a fork, and chill in the freezer for 15 minutes.

To blind-bake the pastry shells, line them with plastic wrap or parchment paper, then fill with pie weights (I use dried lentils) all the way to the top. Bake for 10 minutes, until cooked through, then remove the weights and continue to bake for another 5 minutes, until golden brown. Cool in the pan on a wire rack for 15 minutes. Turn down the oven temperature to 350°F (175°C).

To Finish:

Assorted fresh or candied fruits in hues of orange, yellow, and cream

---

NOTE: *Can sub Raspberry Lambic Jam (page 91) or a good-quality store-bought raspberry jam for a more traditional Bakewell (sprinkle the frangipane with sliced almonds before baking and forgo the glaze for sifted icing sugar). Rhubarb & Amarena Cherry Jam (page 78) would also be delicious (top with a cherry!).*

Spoon 1½ teaspoons of jam into the bottom of each pastry shell, spreading to cover. Divide the frangipane among the tarts (you'll use about 1 tablespoon in each one). Use an offset spatula to spread and level the frangipane, making sure it covers the jam completely. Bake for 15 to 20 minutes, until the tops are puffed and golden. Let cool completely on a wire rack before unmolding.

To make the glaze, place the icing sugar in a bowl with the orange zest and vanilla paste. Add 2 tablespoons of the cream and whisk to combine. Continue adding the cream in small increments, until the glaze is thick but fluid, falling heavily from the whisk. Divide the glaze among the tarts, tipping from side to side to help it cover the tops completely, if necessary.

To finish, decorate the tops with fruit and let the glaze set before serving. These are best eaten fresh but will keep in an airtight container at room temperature for a few days.

This was hands down my favorite recipe of 2016. Its gorgeous color and superlative nature made it an obvious choice to commemorate the late Prince in a small way.

I use plump purple figs, dusty little purple Italian or prune plums, and deep blue coronation grapes, but you can use whatever you like best or can get your hands on most easily. For the most beautiful result, though, do try to stick to the most purplish varieties.

Purple Rain Jam

Makes five 250 mL (8 oz) jars

725 g (3½ cups) stemmed and chopped (½-inch pieces) figs

500 g (2⅓ cups) pitted and chopped (½-inch pieces) plums

425 g (2½ cups) stemmed Coronation grapes

700 g (3½ cups) sugar

75 mL (5 Tbsp) lemon juice

In a large bowl, combine all of the ingredients and let macerate for at least 15 minutes, or up to 1 week, covered, in the refrigerator.

Prepare the jars (see page 20).

Transfer the mixture to a pot or preserving pan. Heat on medium-high and bring to a hard boil, stirring frequently.

When the setting point is reached (see page 23), remove from the heat. Ladle into the prepared jars to within ¼ to ⅛ inch of the rim. Wipe the rims if necessary, seal, and invert for 1 to 2 minutes. Flip right side up and let the jam sit, undisturbed, for 24 hours.

You know that feeling when you come up with something so obvious and delicious that you start to second-guess yourself? Like, since this isn't a thing, it must be because other people already tried and didn't like it? Am I deluded? Well, it's quite possible, but it's hard to imagine anyone not liking vanilla bean crème anglaise treated like panna cotta and set with a little gelatin. It's inspired by the lyric "cold jelly and custard" from "Food, Glorious Food," one of the best songs in one of the best musicals of all time, *Oliver!* And it tastes like ice cream that doesn't melt!

Crème Anglaise Panna Cotta

Makes 875 mL (3½ cups), enough for 6 to 8 individual panna cottas |

125 mL (½ cup) whole milk

134 g (⅔ cup) sugar, divided

1 vanilla bean, split and scraped

8 g (4 sheets) gelatin

140 g (7) egg yolks

500 mL (2 cups) heavy cream

1 jar Purple Rain Jam (page 192)

In a small, heavy-bottomed saucepan over medium heat, combine the milk with half of the sugar and the vanilla bean. Bring just to a simmer and then remove from the heat to steep for 15 to 30 minutes.

In a large bowl, cover the gelatin with cold water to soften.

Bring the milk mixture back to a simmer over medium heat. Meanwhile, in a medium bowl, whisk the yolks with the remaining sugar until they're well combined and a few shades paler. Slowly stream in the hot milk, whisking constantly, then transfer the mixture back to the pot and cook on medium-low heat, stirring constantly, until it reaches 180°F (82°C) on an instant read thermometer or coats the back of a wooden spoon.

Immediately remove from the heat.

NOTE: *Can sub Black Forest Jam (page 172), Tutti Frutti Jam (page 185), a good-quality store-bought fig jam, or . . . honestly there's almost nothing this wouldn't be good with.*

Drain the gelatin sheets, squeezing out any excess water, add to the crème anglaise, and stir until dissolved.

Place the cream in a large measuring jug. Strain the crème anglaise through a fine mesh sieve into the jug with the cream and stir well to combine. Divide the mixture evenly between six to eight ramekins, wide-mouth jars, or teacups—anything cute you have handy really, but about 120 grams (½ cup) per vessel. Carefully transfer them to the refrigerator and let set, uncovered, for at least 4 hours before serving.

To serve, top each panna cotta with one to two spoonfuls of jam.

The panna cottas will keep, covered, for up to 1 week in the refrigerator.

I have been making a variation of this tart for years, matching jams and frangipane flavors with the fruit that I would usually bake right into the top of the tart, where it would sink slightly into the pillow of the frangipane. If you want to go that route—and it's an excellent one—I recommend you use this recipe as a base to do so (just top the frangipane with berries or sliced stone fruit before baking), but if you really want a big visual reward, follow this recipe. The texture and acidity of the raw fruit are nice foils to the rich frangipane and the sweeter, mellower jam. Guests can attempt to get some of everything in each bite, or begin with the "fruit plate" and end with the jam tart. Consider adding quenelles of whipped crème fraîche or barely sweetened mascarpone if you'd really like to take it over the top.

Fruit Plate Frangipane Tart

Makes one 9-inch tart |

1 fully baked Sweet Tart Dough shell (page 230)

⅔ jar Purple Rain Jam (page 192)

1 recipe Frangipane (page 233), substituting ground pistachios for almonds

Enough assorted purple fruit (figs, grapes, plums, etc.) to artfully arrange on top of the tart

---

NOTE: *Can sub Summer Pudding Jam (page 154) (use mixed berries for topping), Tutti Frutti Jam (page 185) (use orange, yellow, and cream fruits for topping), or a good-quality store-bought jam that matches your fruit plate concept.*

Preheat the oven to 350°F (175°C).

Once the baked tart shell has cooled, spread the jam evenly over the bottom of it. Cover with the frangipane, making sure to seal in all of the jam and smoothing the top evenly. Bake for about 25 minutes, until the frangipane is set and golden brown. Let cool completely in the pan on a wire rick.

Remove from the tart pan and place on a serving platter. Artfully arrange fruits on top to resemble a Baroque fruit plate, tearing open figs and spilling grapes over the edge. This will, admittedly, make it slightly difficult to serve, but it will also be very impressive to present, which you should do immediately.

This is best eaten the day it is made, but the unadorned tart can be kept, covered, at room temperature for up to 3 days. Any leftovers topped with fruit can be refrigerated, loosely covered, overnight.

During fall I often want to curl up in a ball and hibernate, at least once I'm done apple picking and eating too many pumpkin treats. So it can be good to inject a little caffeine into the mix. In this jam, the coffee offers a nice bitter counterpoint to sweet, fragrant pears and candy-like dates. Pick plump, sticky dates that taste like caramel, such as Medjool or Deglet Nour. I use kitchen scissors to cut them up to make the job easy. As for the pears, Flemish Beauty or Comice are my pick, but use whatever variety is fresh and fragrant at hand.

Coffee, Date, & Pear Jam

Makes four 250 mL (8 oz) jars

975 g (5½ cups) peeled, cored, and diced pears

500 g (2½ cups) sugar

125 mL (½ cup) crabapple juice (page 63) (optional)

45 mL (3 Tbsp) lemon juice

200 g (1 cup lightly packed) pitted dates, quartered

190 mL (¾ cup) hot, strong coffee

1 tsp ground coffee

In a large bowl, combine the pears with the sugar, crabapple juice, if using, and lemon juice, and let macerate overnight, or for up to 1 week, covered, in the refrigerator.

In a small bowl, cover the dates with the hot coffee. Cover the dish with plastic wrap and soak for at least 3 hours, or up to overnight.

Prepare the jars (see page 20).

Transfer the pear mixture to a pot or preserving pan and add the coffee-soaked dates, along with any remaining soaking liquid. Heat on medium-high and bring to a hard boil, stirring frequently.

When the setting point is reached (see page 23), remove from the heat and mix in the ground coffee. Ladle into the prepared jars to within ¼ to ⅛ inch of the rim. Remove any air bubbles, wipe the rims if necessary, seal, and invert for 1 to 2 minutes. Flip right side up and let the jam sit, undisturbed, for 24 hours.

Financiers are little French cakes, rich with almonds and brown butter, traditionally baked in shallow rectangular pans that make them look like gold bars, hence the name. Tragically, I do not own these pans, but probably neither do you, so likely it's for the best that this recipe bakes them in regular old muffin tins. If you do have them, however, feel free to use them. Or use mini muffin pans for a petit four, or a 9½-inch springform pan to make a cake instead. Just decrease or increase the baking time depending on the size. No matter what pan you use, though, you'll be rewarded with a rich, deeply hazelnutty, crisp on the outside and moist on the inside cake that pairs spectacularly well with the pear jam.

Hazelnut Financiers

Makes 12 financiers |

150 g (⅔ cup) Brown Butter (page 228)

160 g (1⅓ cups) toasted hazelnuts or toasted ground hazelnuts

160 g (1¼ cups) icing sugar, plus extra for dusting (dusting optional)

50 g (⅓ cup + 1 Tbsp) ground almonds

47 g (⅓ cup) all-purpose flour

1 tsp espresso powder

½ tsp salt

150 g (5) egg whites, at room temperature

⅓ jar Coffee, Date, & Pear Jam (page 198)

In a small pot, or in a bowl in the microwave (for 45 seconds to 1 minute), melt the brown butter. Cover to keep warm.

In a food processor fitted with the steel blade, pulse the toasted hazelnuts and icing sugar until finely ground. Sift this mixture with the ground almonds, flour, espresso powder, and salt into a bowl. Whisk in the egg whites—the mixture will be quite stiff. Gradually whisk in the warm brown butter until combined. Cover with plastic wrap, making sure it touches the surface of the mixture, and refrigerate for at least 4 hours, or up to 3 days.

Preheat the oven to 350°F (175°C). Generously grease 12 muffin cups with butter. Divide the batter evenly between the cups (I use the no. 20 yellow scoop). Once you've filled each cup, make a depression in the center of each with your fingers. Fill each with a generous teaspoon of jam.

Bake for about 30 minutes, until golden brown around the edges. Let cool in the pan on a wire rack for at least 10 minutes before eating. If desired, dust with icing sugar before serving.

Financiers are best eaten the day they are made and the batter keeps well in the refrigerator or freezer, so I suggest only baking as many as you want to serve that day. If you do have any leftovers, they can be stored in an airtight container at room temperature for up to 2 days.

On my first day of pastry school in Montreal, I was petrified. I had passed the French exam to gain admittance (it was, bizarrely, a reading comprehension of an article on acid rain), but I was not confident in my abilities to understand or be understood by my teachers and fellow students. In the locker room after class, a sweet, confident girl introduced herself to me as Stephanie Labelle and told me she spoke English and would be happy to help me anytime I needed. In the end, I learned not only pastry skills at school but also to speak French fluently—sometimes even now I can't remember pastry words in English. More importantly, though, I made a friend for life. Steph was top of the class, left for Paris to work with Pierre Hermé, and went on to open one of Montreal's best pastry shops, Pâtisserie Rhubarbe. This is her excellent recipe for the classic Basque cake—rich buckwheat sablé Breton dough encasing a filling of pastry cream and, in this case, Coffee, Date, & Pear Jam.

Gâteau Basque

Makes one 9-inch cake |

For the Sablé Breton:

300 g (2 cups + 2 Tbsp) all-purpose flour

150 g (1¼ cups) buckwheat flour

1 Tbsp baking powder

¾ tsp salt

160 g (8) egg yolks

320 g (1½ cups + 1½ Tbsp) sugar

320 g (1⅓ cups + 1 Tbsp) unsalted butter, softened

For the Filling:

1 recipe Pastry Cream (page 229)

1 jar Coffee, Date, & Pear Jam (page 198)

1 recipe Egg Wash (page 229)

To make the sablé Breton dough, in a small bowl, combine both flours, the baking powder, and salt. Set aside.

In a stand mixer fitted with the whisk attachment, whip the yolks with the sugar on high speed until the ribbon stage, when the mixture is pale and thick and leaves ribbon-like trails that take a moment to sink back in when the mixture is lifted. Switch to the paddle attachment, add the dry ingredients, and mix on low just to combine. Add the butter and mix on low just until combined. Divide the dough into two halves, wrap in plastic, and refrigerate for at least 1 hour, until firm.

NOTE: *Can sub Black Currant &*
Sweet Cherry Jam (page 96), Bombe
Matin Marmalade (page 215),
Cranberry & Clementine Jam
(page 118), or a good-quality store-
bought pear jam.

Grease an 8½-inch springform pan with butter or nonstick spray. Roll out one disk of dough to ¼ inch thick and cut out a 10-inch circle. Fit this into the bottom and up the sides of the pan. Fill with the pastry cream, then layer the jam on top. Using a pastry brush, brush some egg wash onto the edges of the crust.

Roll out the second disk of dough to ¼ inch thick and cut out an 8½-inch circle. Place this on top of the jam, pressing on the edges so it adheres to the bottom crust. Refrigerate for at least 1 hour, or up to overnight.

Preheat the oven to 350°F (175°C).

Brush the top of the cake with the egg wash, then use the back of a paring knife to trace diagonal lines to form a diamond pattern on the surface, but without cutting all the way through the pastry.

Bake for about 1 hour and 30 minutes, until deeply golden brown and an instant read thermometer poked into the middle reads 210°F (99°C). Let cool completely in the pan on a wire rack before serving.

Basque cake is best the day it is made, but any leftovers can be kept in an airtight container at room temperature overnight.

When I'm sick I make myself a soothing hot drink. Thing is, it's so good I kind of want it all the time in the winter. Well, here it is reborn in beautiful, quivering, crystalline jelly form, with bits of candied ginger. You can savor it on a scone with thick cream, or you can stir it into hot water for an instant feeling of being cared for. I used to use bourbon for this jelly, but now I tend toward a smoky blended scotch. Whatever whisky you have will likely do the trick (or omit if you prefer).

Rhume Rx Jelly

Makes five 250 mL (8 oz) jars

500 g (4) lemons

500 g (2½ cups) sugar

340 g (1 cup) honey

250 mL (1 cup) lemon juice

50 g (2-inch) piece fresh ginger, peeled and finely grated

65 g (⅓ cup + 1 Tbsp) diced candied ginger

1½ Tbsp whisky

2 pinches of cayenne

Wash the lemons, remove the ends, thinly slice, and place them, seeds and all, in a large pot with 1.5 liters (6 cups) of water. Bring to a boil over high heat, turn down the heat to medium, and simmer, uncovered, for 30 minutes. Remove from the heat, let rest for 30 minutes, then strain through a jelly bag or fine mesh sieve set over a deep bowl. Let it drip overnight.

The next day, prepare the jars (see page 20).

Combine the strained lemon liquid (discard the solids) with the sugar, honey, lemon juice, and fresh ginger in a large pot or preserving pan over medium-high heat. Bring to a boil, add the candied ginger, and boil hard, stirring occasionally. When the setting point is reached (see page 23), remove from the heat and add the whisky and cayenne. Pour into the prepared jars to within ¼ to ⅛ inch of the rim. Wipe the rims if necessary, seal, and invert for 1 to 2 minutes. Flip right side up and let the jam sit, undisturbed, for 24 hours.

Recipe pictured on page 209

This is my take on a slightly obscure but very delicious bar cookie from Scotland. If you like buttery shortbread, sugar, and spicy ginger, this is for you. This keeps well and is an excellent accompaniment to black tea.

Ginger Crunch

Makes 25 squares |

For the Base:

175 g (1¼ cups) all-purpose flour

38 g (3 Tbsp) sugar

1 tsp baking powder

1 tsp ground ginger

½ tsp salt

Zest of ½ lemon

115 g (½ cup) unsalted butter, cold, cubed

For the Topping:

86 g (6 Tbsp) unsalted butter

125 g (1 cup) icing sugar

¾ tsp ground ginger

Pinch of salt

45 mL (3 Tbsp) Rhume Rx Jelly (page 205)

———————

NOTE: *Can sub good-quality store-bought ginger marmalade or shredded lemon marmalade.*

———————

Preheat the oven to 350°F (175°C). Grease an 8-inch square pan with butter or nonstick spray and line with parchment paper.

To make the base, in a medium bowl, combine the flour, sugar, baking powder, ground ginger, salt, and lemon zest. Add the butter and use your fingertips to rub it in until the mixture is sandy and clumps together when pressed. Press evenly into the pan.

Bake for 25 to 30 minutes, until golden brown.

About 5 minutes before the base is ready, make the topping. In a small pot over medium heat, melt the butter. Whisk in the icing sugar, ground ginger, salt, and jelly. Bring to a boil, stirring constantly. Boil for 30 seconds then remove from the heat and immediately pour over the base when it comes out of the oven. Let cool in the pan on a wire rack before cutting into squares. The squares will keep in an airtight container at room temperature for at least 1 week.

When I first heard about this pie, I was in my early 20s, and I felt cheated that I hadn't been eating it my whole life. It's basically a marmalade pie, which is my truest dream. This version adds an intriguing extra layer of flavor thanks to the Rhume Rx (page 205)—a little ginger, a hint of whisky. Might I suggest you enjoy it with a hot toddy?

Shaker Lemon Pie

Serves 8 to 10 servings |

350 g (2 large) lemons

350 g (1¾ cups) sugar

½ jar Rhume Rx Jelly (page 205)

¼ tsp salt

1 recipe Galette Dough (double crust) (page 232)

4 large eggs, at room temperature

58 g (¼ cup) unsalted butter, melted

35 g (¼ cup) all-purpose flour

Milk, for brushing

Wash, halve, and slice the lemons into rounds as thinly as possible, disposing of the stem end and any seeds. In a large bowl, combine the sliced lemons, the sugar, jelly, and salt. Cover and let stand overnight at room temperature, stirring a few times to make sure all of the citrus is evenly sugared.

The next day, preheat the oven to 400°F (200°C). Grease a 9-inch pie plate with butter or nonstick spray.

On a lightly floured surface, roll one disk of dough into a circle about 12 inches in diameter. Fold it into quarters, brushing off any excess flour, and place it in one-quarter of the pie plate. Unfold the dough and press down on it to remove any air bubbles hiding underneath. Refrigerate, uncovered, until ready to use.

In a medium bowl, whisk the eggs until blended, then whisk in the butter, followed by the flour. Add the lemon mixture, and use a spatula to fold it in. Pour the lemon filling into the dough-lined pie plate.

NOTE: *Can sub A Different Seville Marmalade (page 70) (sub Seville oranges for some or all of the lemons) or a good-quality store-bought lemon marmalade.*

Roll out the second galette dough disk to a circle 12 inches in diameter. Brush the exposed edges of the bottom crust with a little cold water then gently set the top crust over it. Press down around the edges so it adheres, then use kitchen scissors or a paring knife to trim away any excess dough, leaving a 1-inch overhang all the way around. Tuck the dough under and crimp the edges. Brush the pie with milk and cut a few slits on top to let the steam escape. Place the pie on a rimmed baking sheet to catch any juice that might bubble over.

Bake for 30 to 35 minutes, until brown, then turn down the oven temperature to 350°F (175°C) and continue to bake for another 35 to 40 minutes, until thick juices bubble up from the steam vents. Let cool completely in the pan on a wire rack before serving.

Pie is best the day it is made, but any leftovers can be kept at room temperature, covered with foil, for up to 3 days.

[left to right] Rhume Rx Jelly (page 205), Shaker Lemon Pie (page 207)

What could be a better welcome to a holiday party than the rich, tantalizing smell of mulled wine? Any time of year, this marmalade invokes that feeling. And what could be a better use for the bottles of red wine of uncertain vintage inevitably left behind after a holiday party?

Mulled Wine Marmalade

Makes five to six 250 mL (8 oz) jars

480 g (5–6) clementines

120 g (1 small) lemon

1 (750 mL) bottle fruity red wine (see note)

600 g (3 cups) sugar

255 g (¾ cup) honey

60 mL (¼ cup) lemon juice

2-inch piece cinnamon stick

1 star anise

4 cloves

4 allspice berries

A few blades of mace

2 Tbsp port, brandy, or Calvados (optional)

NOTE: *Just as with a batch of mulled wine, you don't want to use great wine, but you don't want anything undrinkable either.*

Wash the clementines and lemon, slice off the ends, quarter the fruit lengthwise, and cut it into ¼-inch-thick slices, discarding any seeds. In a large pot, combine the sliced fruit with the wine and 750 mL (3 cups) water. Leave to soak, covered, overnight (but no longer) at room temperature.

The next day, bring the mixture to a boil, uncovered, over high heat. Turn down the heat and simmer until the citrus peel is very soft and the liquid has reduced by two-thirds. This will take about 1 hour.

Prepare the jars (see page 20).

Add the sugar, honey, and lemon juice to the cooked citrus mixture. Put the spices into a large metal tea ball or muslin bag and throw it into the pot. Heat on medium-high and bring to a hard boil, stirring frequently.

When the setting point is reached (page 23), remove from the heat and add the port, if using. Pour into the prepared jars to within ¼ to ⅛ inch of the rim. Remove any air bubbles, wipe the rims if necessary, seal, and invert for 1 to 2 minutes. Flip right side up and let the jam sit, undisturbed, for 24 hours.

Roasted Pears (page 212)

I first made this recipe shortly after Christmas, and I cannot explain what a sublime relief it was to just eat baked fruit after so much flour, sugar, butter, and eggs. This really hits the spot regardless of when you eat it, though. It's reserved enough for breakfast but elegant enough for a dinner party. Pair it with ice cream, custard, or just a glug of heavy cream or a spoonful of thick yogurt. Me? I like these pears best served warm, with some of their thick syrup spooned on top and caught in the cavity left by the core. Simpler delights, there are few.

Roasted Pears

Serves 5 to 6 |

½ jar Mulled Wine Marmalade (page 210)

Juice of 1 orange

2 Tbsp honey

2–3 coins of fresh ginger

850 g (5–6) just ripe pears (any type)

2 Tbsp unsalted butter

NOTE: *Can sub A Different Seville Marmalade (page 70), Rhume Rx Jelly (page 205), or a good-quality store-bought marmalade (but none of them will be as festive!).*

Preheat the oven to 375°F (190°C). Grease a 9- x 13-inch pan with butter or nonstick spray.

Place the marmalade, orange juice, honey, and ginger in the pan and stir to combine.

Peel the pears, halve them lengthwise, and use a melon baller (or round metal teaspoon) to neatly remove their cores. I like to leave the stems, but you can remove them with a paring knife if you prefer.

Place the pears cut side down in the pan and dot them with the butter.

Bake for 45 minutes to 1 hour, basting every 15 minutes, until the syrup is thick and the cut sides of the pears are lightly caramelized.

Serve immediately, or transfer to an airtight container while the syrup is still fluid and cooperative and store in the refrigerator for up to 1 week.

Recipe pictured on page 211

If you're looking for a showstopping holiday dessert, here it is. Trifle is a traditional Christmas offering, but rarely is it this good. Yes, there are a few components, but it's easy to make the gingerbread ahead and freeze it, and the pears can be made a few days in advance as well. And after the fact, I think any leftovers make an excellent, if decadent, breakfast.

I finally bought a trifle bowl—a footed, straight-sided glass receptacle that best displays the dessert. If you don't have one, any medium-large decorative bowl will do the job, or you could get fancy and make individual trifles layered in glasses.

Trifle

Serves 12 | 𝄎𝄎𝄎

For the Base:

½ recipe Gingerbread (page 224), using Mulled Wine Marmalade (page 210) and omitting the glaze

1 recipe Roasted Pears (page 212)

For the Custard:

560 mL (2¼ cups) heavy cream

120 g (6) egg yolks

50 g (¼ cup) sugar

2½ tsp cornstarch

Pinch of salt

2½ tsp sweet sherry

NOTE: *Can sub A Different Seville Marmalade (page 70) or a good-quality store-bought orange marmalade.*

Once the gingerbread and roasted pears are ready, place them both in the refrigerator until ready to assemble.

To make the custard, in a medium pot over medium heat, warm the cream. While it warms, in a medium bowl, whisk together the yolks, sugar, cornstarch, and salt until well combined. When the cream is almost at a boil, pour it slowly into the yolks, whisking constantly. Transfer the mixture back to the pot and cook on medium-low, stirring constantly, until thickened. Be careful not to overcook it. Pour the mixture through a fine mesh sieve into a bowl, stir in the sherry, and cover with plastic wrap directly on the surface. Let cool at room temperature.

While the custard cools, cut the gingerbread horizontally into two layers and sandwich them together with the marmalade. Cut into 1- to 1½-inch cubes and arrange in the bottom of your trifle bowl. Sprinkle the sherry over top.

To Assemble:

330 mL (1⅓ cups) heavy cream

60 mL (¼ cup) sweet sherry

Seeds of ½ pomegranate

2 Tbsp toasted sliced or slivered
almonds

Slice the pear halves into quarters and place them, plus any syrup from the container, on top of the ginger-bread. Pour the custard over the pears. Cover and refrigerate for at least 2 hours, or up to overnight.

To assemble, in a stand mixer fitted with the whisk attachment, whip the cream with the sherry on medium-high speed to firm peaks and spread evenly over the top of the trifle. Garnish with pomegranate seeds and almonds.

It's a weird name for a marmalade, yes. The joke is that it sort of sounds like "good morning" in French (*bon matin!*), referring to the coffee in the recipe, but it actually means "morning bomb," referring to the whisky. Listen, jokes are never good when you have to explain them. Just trust me, it sounds cool in French. What's important here is that bitter oranges, coffee, and whisky are a match made in heaven.

Bombe Matin Marmalade

Makes seven 250 mL (8 oz) jars

800 g (about 4½) Seville oranges

1.2 kg (6 cups) sugar

75 mL (5 Tbsp) whisky, divided

60 mL (¼ cup) lemon juice

2 Tbsp coffee beans

¾ tsp ground coffee

Wash the oranges, slice off the ends, quarter the oranges lengthwise, and cut them into ⅛-inch-thick slices. Place the orange slices in a large bowl, cover with 2 liters (8 cups) of water, and leave to soak overnight (but no longer).

The next day, in a large pot, bring the oranges and water to a boil. Turn down the heat and simmer, uncovered, until the oranges are very soft and the mixture has reduced by about two-thirds, about 1 hour.

Prepare the jars (see page 20).

Add the sugar, half the whisky, and the lemon juice to the cooked oranges. Put the coffee beans into a large tea ball or muslin bag, and add to the pot. Heat on medium-high and bring to a hard boil, stirring frequently.

When the setting point is reached (see page 23), remove from the heat and add the ground coffee, stirring well to combine. Pour into the prepared jars to within ¼ to ⅛ inch of the rim. Wipe the rims if necessary, seal, and invert for 1 to 2 minutes. Flip right side up and let the marmalade sit, undisturbed, for 24 hours.

Rugelach is a delicious and flaky blank canvas upon which to experiment. Feel free to embellish this recipe—sprinkle chocolate or nuts over the marmalade, mix some ground espresso into the sugar for sprinkling—or depart from it entirely. You can substitute the rye flour with another flour, cover the dough in any sort of jam or caramel or fudge as you please . . . We changed the filling almost every batch at a bakery I used to work at, and it seemed impossible to go wrong.

Rugelach

Makes 32 rugelach |

230 g (1 cup) unsalted butter, cold, cubed

230 g (one 8 oz package) cream cheese, cold, cubed

140 g (1 cup) all-purpose flour

140 g (1 cup) whole rye flour

½ tsp salt

1 jar Bombe Matin Marmalade (page 215)

1 recipe Egg Wash (page 229)

Sugar, for finishing

NOTE: *Can sub Prune & Meyer Lemon Butter (page 145), Dried Apricot & Verjus Butter (page 132), A Different Seville Marmalade (page 70), or your favorite good-quality store-bought jam or marmalade.*

In a stand mixer fitted with the paddle attachment, mix the butter and cream cheese with both flours and the salt on medium-low speed until the dough comes together in a rough mass. Divide the dough in half and form each half into a disk. Wrap and chill in the refrigerator for at least 30 minutes. (Or freeze for up to 1 month and bring to cool room temperature before using.)

Preheat the oven to 325°F (160°C). Line a baking sheet with parchment paper.

On a floured surface, turn out one disk of dough and roll it into a circle 16 inches in diameter. Trim any rough edges with a paring knife, then spread about half the marmalade over the surface. Cut the dough into 16 equally sized triangles and roll each one up, starting at the wide end, into a little crescent. Place on the baking sheet, at least 1 inch apart, brush with egg wash, and sprinkle with sugar (or dip them into a shallow bowl of each). Repeat with the second disk of dough.

Bake for about 40 minutes, until deep golden brown. Let cool completely on the pan on a wire rack before serving.

These are best eaten the day they are made. They also freeze very well and bake well from frozen, so you may prepare them in advance but only bake them on the day they're needed. That said, probably no one will complain too much if you give them a day-old rugelach.

When I was growing up, these were my absolute favorite cookies. My grandmother would make them around the holidays and keep them in tins in the freezer. I remember my cousin David liked them particularly when they were still partially frozen, but I liked them any way I could get them. They have a buttery, melting shortbread base topped with a thick layer of dulce de leche–like caramel (that's the sweetened condensed milk) and blanketed with bittersweet chocolate, which cuts the sugar (a little). I grew up in Alberta, Canada, and had no idea these weren't my grandmother's invention. They're titled Granny's Shortbread Squares on the sheet of paper where I copied the recipe down. Turns out they're a very popular cookie in the UK called millionaire's shortbread, but I have yet to meet a better version than hers—although nostalgia may play some part in that. Of course, I've gone and doctored it up here with coffee and oranges, which add aroma and a little bitterness (my favorite) to balance the sugar.

Millionaire's Shortbread

Makes 25 squares |

For the Base:

140 g (1 cup) all-purpose flour

50 g (¼ cup) sugar

Zest of ½ orange

½ tsp ground espresso

Pinch of salt

115 g (½ cup) unsalted butter, cold, cubed

Preheat the oven to 350°F (175°C). Grease an 8-inch square pan with butter or nonstick spray and line with parchment paper.

In a medium bowl, whisk together the flour, sugar, orange zest, espresso, and salt. Use your fingertips to rub in the butter until the mixture is crumbly and there are no pieces of butter visible. Press the mixture firmly and evenly into the prepared pan. Bake for about 30 minutes, until golden brown. Let cool completely in the pan on a wire rack.

For the Caramel:

115 g (½ cup) unsalted butter

110 g (½ cup) brown sugar

1 (300 mL/14 oz) tin sweetened
    condensed milk

2 Tbsp Bombe Matin Marmalade
    (page 215)

Pinch of salt

For the Topping:

172 g (6 oz) dark chocolate

43 g (3 Tbsp) butter

1 Tbsp Bombe Matin Marmalade
    (page 215), finely chopped

———————

NOTE: *Can sub A Different Seville
Marmalade (page 70) or a good-quality
store-bought Seville orange marmalade.*

———————

To make the caramel, in a medium pot, cook the butter, brown sugar, condensed milk, marmalade, and salt over medium heat, stirring to melt the butter and dissolve the sugar. When it comes to a simmer, turn down the heat to medium-low and cook, stirring constantly (this scorches VERY easily), for about 7 minutes, until the mixture is thick and tan-colored. Pour this caramel onto the shortbread base, tilting the pan for even coverage. Let cool completely at room temperature.

To make the topping, in a heatproof bowl, combine the chocolate, butter, and chopped marmalade. Either microwave in 15-second bursts, stirring in between each one, until melted, or set over a pot of simmering water, stirring until melted. Pour the melted chocolate over the caramel, using an offset spatula to cover it evenly. Let the chocolate set, at room temperature, before cutting into squares. You may need to throw it in the refrigerator to help the caramel firm up to cut, but if you do that, you'll also have to use a hot knife to cut the chocolate cleanly (just run the knife under hot water then dry it with a clean kitchen towel between each cut).

These keep well in an airtight container at room temperature for up to 5 days. They also freeze beautifully in an airtight container or wrapped in wax paper and foil for up to 2 months.

I'm not trying to start anything, but as far as cocktails go, the Dark & Stormy is far superior to the Moscow Mule. Both are made with ginger beer and lime, and sure it's pretty cool that the Moscow Mule is served in an eponymous copper mug. But I'm here for what's in the cup, and the Dark & Stormy's dark rum brings so much more than vodka ever could. The molasses and caramel flavors amplify the ginger and act as a foil to the lime. That's why this isn't a Moscow Mule marmalade.

Dark & Stormy Marmalade

Makes five to six 250 mL (8 oz) jars

600 g (6) limes

600 g (3 cups) sugar

330 g (1½ cups) brown sugar

50 g (2-inch piece) fresh ginger, peeled and finely grated

1 tsp ground ginger

60 mL (¼ cup) lime or lemon juice

3 Tbsp dark rum (optional) (see note)

½ tsp citric acid

———————

NOTE: *If you don't like or drink rum, feel free to omit it—you'll still have a delicious lime and ginger concoction.*

———————

Wash the limes, slice off the ends, quarter the limes lengthwise, and slice them into ¼-inch-thick triangles. Place them in a large pot, cover with 1.5 liters (6 cups) water, cover, and leave to soak overnight (but no longer).

The next day, bring to a boil over high heat. Turn down the heat and simmer, uncovered, until the peels are very soft and the mixture has reduced by about two-thirds. This will take about 1 hour.

Prepare the jars (see page 20).

Add both sugars, both gingers, and the lime juice to the cooked limes. Heat on medium-high and bring to a hard boil, stirring frequently.

When the setting point is reached (see page 23), remove from the heat and add the rum and citric acid, stirring well to combine. Pour into the prepared jars to within ¼ to ⅛ inch of the rim. Remove any air bubbles, wipe the rims if necessary, seal, and invert for 1 to 2 minutes. Flip right side up and let the marmalade sit, undisturbed, for 24 hours.

Fruitcake can be controversial, but as I wrote in my first book, I think that's because most people have never had a good one, and I'm convinced a good one can make a convert out of a fruitcake skeptic. As a fruitcake lover, though, I was a little surprised when I first tasted my new experiment—I missed the sticky molasses, the gingerbread quality. Once I shook off my expectations and preconceptions, however, I realized that this white fruitcake is a winner. It might even convince a few recalcitrant fruitcake haters. Stopping at one slice is difficult, so you might consider making a double batch. It does keep incredibly well, after all. For the best result, make this at least a month before you intend to serve it.

Tropical Fruitcake

Makes two 6-inch round cakes |

80 g (½ cup) golden raisins

90 g (½ cup) pitted and chopped dates

65 g (½ cup) chopped dried mango

100 g (½ cup) chopped candied
    pineapple

40 g (¼ cup) chopped candied ginger

1 jar Dark & Stormy Marmalade
    (page 221)

80 mL (⅓ cup) golden rum,
    plus more for dousing

210 g (1½ cups) all-purpose flour

½ tsp baking powder

¼ tsp baking soda

¼ tsp salt

1 tsp ground ginger

½ tsp freshly grated nutmeg

The day before you plan to bake your fruitcakes, in a big bowl, stir together the dried and candied fruit, ginger, marmalade, and rum. Cover and let sit overnight.

The next day, preheat the oven to 350°F (175°C). Grease two 6-inch round pans with butter and line with parchment.

In a medium bowl, whisk together the flour, baking powder, baking soda, salt, ginger, nutmeg, and allspice.

In a stand mixer fitted with the paddle attachment, cream the butter and sugar on medium speed until light and fluffy. Add the clementine zest and juice, beating to combine. Add the eggs one at a time, mixing well between each addition.

¼ tsp ground allspice

115 g (½ cup) unsalted butter,
   at room temperature

220 g (1 cup) brown sugar

Zest and juice of 1 clementine

2 large eggs, at room temperature

80 g (½ cup) Brazil nuts

60 g (½ cup) cashews

25 g (½ cup) flaked unsweetened
   coconut

125 mL (½ cup) golden rum

NOTE: *Can sub A Different Seville Marmalade (page 70) or a good-quality store-bought lime and/or ginger marmalade.*

Add the flour mixture and mix on low until just combined. Finally, fold in the fruit mixture, nuts, and coconut. Divide the batter evenly between the two pans.

Bake for about 1 hour, until golden brown and a toothpick comes out with just a few moist crumbs attached.

Let cool in the pans on a wire rack for 20 minutes before removing the cakes from their pans and letting cool completely.

When they're cool, cut two multilayered pieces of cheesecloth big enough to wrap a cake. Put them in a bowl and pour on half the golden rum, soaking the cheesecloth. Wring out one piece, swaddle a cake in it, and wrap the cake in a layer of aluminum foil lined with wax paper. Repeat with the second cake.

Store the cakes somewhere cool and dark. Every week, peel back the foil and wax paper to sprinkle some more rum over the top of the cakes. This is called feeding your cakes. You can serve them after 1 month of feeding, but they'll last up to 1 year if you keep feeding them every month or so.

Serve in thin slices.

Get ready for your whole house to smell like Christmas, but with a tropical twist. This loaf is striking—deep brown with a bright white glaze and flecks of green lime zest. Besides its looks and its heavenly fragrance, its virtues include being very easy to make, keeping particularly well, and being versatile to boot—it is just as good at tea time as it is for dessert with a big spoonful of whipped cream and a glass of rum alongside, or as an essential building block to the trifle on page 213.

Gingerbread

Serves 8 to 10 |

For the Gingerbread Loaf:

350 g (2½ cups) all-purpose flour

1 tsp baking powder

1 tsp baking soda

1 tsp Mixed Spice (page 233)

½ tsp salt

100 g (½ cup) sugar

2 large eggs, at room temperature

80 mL (⅓ cup) heavy cream

45 mL (3 Tbsp) neutral oil

1 Tbsp grated fresh ginger
   (about one 2-inch knob)

250 mL (1 cup) hot black tea

160 g (½ cup) molasses

½ jar Dark & Stormy Marmalade
   (page 221)

Preheat the oven to 350°F (175°C). Grease a 5- x 9-inch loaf pan with butter or nonstick spray and line with parchment paper.

To make the gingerbread loaf, in a bowl, whisk together the flour, baking powder, baking soda, mixed spice, and salt.

In a larger bowl, whisk together the sugar and eggs. Whisk in the cream, oil, and ginger.

In a large measuring cup, use a fork or whisk to combine the tea, molasses, and marmalade.

Mix one-third of the flour mixture into the sugar mixture, add half the tea mixture, and mix to combine. Repeat until everything is incorporated.

Pour into the prepared pan and bake for about 1 hour, until an instant read thermometer inserted in the center reads 210°F (99°C), or a toothpick inserted in the center comes out with just a few moist crumbs attached.

For the Glaze:

2 Tbsp butter, melted

2 Tbsp dark rum

125 g (1 cup) icing sugar

Zest of 1 lime

NOTE: *Can sub Mulled Wine Marmalade (page 210), A Different Seville Marmalade (page 70), or a good-quality store-bought lime and/or ginger marmalade.*

Let the gingerbread cool in the pan on a wire rack for 30 minutes. Remove from the pan and let cool completely.

To make the glaze, in a small bowl, whisk the melted butter and rum into the icing sugar until smooth and pourable. Place the gingerbread on a wire rack set over a rimmed baking sheet or a length of wax paper. Pour the glaze evenly over the loaf, using a spatula to nudge it over the edges if need be. Scatter the lime zest all over the top. Let set before slicing and serving.

BASE
RECIPES

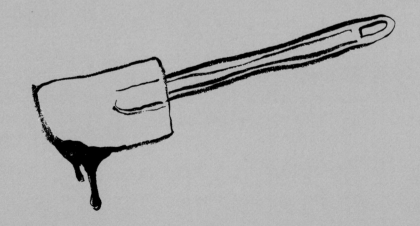

Brown Butter

Makes 400 g (1¾ cups)

I first encountered brown butter at pastry school. It was so incredible that I worried I might have wasted the first 20 years of my life without it. An essential ingredient in some pastries like financiers (page 199), it's generally great to use anywhere you're using butter. I like to make a whole block of it at once and keep it at the ready, like we do in professional pastry kitchens. It's a wonderful thing to have on hand.

454 g (1 lb) unsalted butter

Have a heatproof container at the ready.

Cut the butter into chunks and place them in a medium saucepan. Melt over medium-high heat and cook, stirring occasionally, until the foam subsides and the butter smells like toffee and toasted nuts. (Keep an eye on it, as it can burn quickly.) There will be brown caramelized milk solids on the bottom of the pan.

Immediately remove from the heat and transfer to the heatproof container. Let cool to room temperature before using or refrigerating for future use. It will keep for up to 2 weeks in an airtight container in the refrigerator.

Pastry Cream
Makes 500 mL (2 cups)

Pastry cream is one of the first things I learned to make at pastry school. It's like a very thick custard, used to fill tarts and donuts, and the base for many other pastry fillings.

375 mL (1½ cups) whole milk

100 g (5) egg yolks

100 g (½ cup) sugar

24 g (3 Tbsp) cornstarch

1 Tbsp all-purpose flour

43 g (3 Tbsp) unsalted butter, cold and cubed

1½ tsp vanilla extract

In a medium pot over medium-high heat, heat the milk until it's almost at a boil.

In the meantime, in a bowl, whisk the egg yolks with the sugar, cornstarch, and flour.

While you whisk, in a slow and steady stream, pour the milk into the yolk mixture. When it's all incorporated, return to the pot and cook, whisking, over medium heat. When it comes to a thick boil, continue whisking for about 30 seconds, then remove from the heat.

Strain through a fine mesh sieve into a heatproof bowl to remove any lumpy bits, then whisk in the butter and vanilla. Place a sheet of plastic wrap directly on the surface so a skin doesn't form and let cool completely. Refrigerate until ready to use. Pastry cream will keep for up to 2 days in an airtight container in the refrigerator.

Egg Wash
Makes 2 Tbsp

Egg wash is used to give baked goods sheen and a golden color. There are a few different ways to make it, but none are as rich and sublime as that of my friend Michelle Marek.

1 egg yolk

1 Tbsp heavy cream

In a small bowl, whisk together the yolk and cream.

Egg wash keeps up to 5 days in an airtight container in the refrigerator.

Sweet Tart Dough

Makes one 9-inch tart shell

This is a gorgeous, crisp, cookie-like crust that you'll want to use for your fruit tarts. The warmer the dough is, though, the more difficult it is to handle, so just let it temper enough that you can roll it and no more. That said, if all else fails, you can just press it into the tart pan as evenly as possible. Or patch it carefully if things go awry.

185 g (¾ cup + 1 Tbsp) unsalted butter, softened

42 g (⅓ cup) icing sugar

¼ tsp salt

210 g (1½ cups) all-purpose flour

4 tsp heavy cream

In a stand mixer fitted with the paddle attachment, beat the butter with the sugar and salt on medium speed until well combined and fluffy. Add the flour and mix on low speed until it's mostly incorporated. Add the cream and mix on low speed until the dough comes together.

On a lightly floured work surface, turn out the dough and smoosh it a few times with the heel of your hand to really make it homogeneous—no corner should be crumbly or dry. Form the dough into a disk, wrap it in plastic, and refrigerate for at least 1 hour, or up to 3 days. (Or freeze it for up to 2 months. Thaw it in the refrigerator and bring to room temperature before using.)

To blind-bake, preheat the oven to 375°F (190°C). Let the dough rest at room temperature for about 15 minutes. Grease a 9-inch tart pan with butter, then roll out the dough to ⅛ inch thick. Either roll it up on your rolling pin and unroll it over the pan, or fold it into quarters and unfold it in the pan. Either way, use a pastry brush to dust off any excess flour as you go. Snuggle the dough into the sides of the pan and trim the edges flush with its sides. Refrigerate for at least 30 minutes, or up to overnight.

When you're ready to bake, dock the dough by piercing it repeatedly with a fork over the bottoms and sides. This will help eliminate any bubbling. Line the tart shell with plastic wrap, then fill to the top with pie weights or dried beans (I use lentils). Bake for 20 minutes, then carefully remove the plastic wrap and pie weights, and continue to bake for 5 minutes, until fully cooked (with no raw patches of dough) but not fully browned. Proceed with recipe as directed.

To fully bake, follow the instructions for blind-baking, but continue to bake until the entire crust is golden brown. This will take about 5 minutes longer. Let cool completely before using.

Galette Dough

Makes one 9-inch crust or two 9-inch crusts

Technically this dough is for a rustic open-face tart called a galette, so it really only exists in that sense as a single-crust recipe, but I love how flaky and nice it is, so I use it for tarts, hand pies, and pies. Sue me. I have provided two recipes, one for a single crust (with variations for some of the other recipes in this book) and one for a double crust.

Single Crust:

280 g (2 cups) all-purpose flour (see note)

1 tsp sugar

¾ tsp salt

200 g (¾ cup + 2 Tbsp) unsalted butter, cold, cubed (see note)

4–6 Tbsp ice water

Double Crust:

420 g (3 cups) all-purpose flour

1½ tsp sugar

1 tsp salt (heaping)

230 g (1 cup) unsalted butter, cold, cubed

70 g (⅓ cup) lard, cold, cubed

6–9 Tbsp ice water

In a stand mixer fitted with the paddle attachment, mix together the flour, sugar, salt, butter, and lard, if using, on medium-low speed until the butter is variously the size of olives and peas. If necessary, stop the mixer and squish any large pieces between your thumb and forefinger. With the mixer running on low, add the ice water 1 tablespoon at a time, until the dough begins to come together. Let it run a few more seconds, then stop and press the dough into a disk. If you're making a double crust, divide the dough into two disks. Wrap the dough in plastic and refrigerate for 30 minutes to 1 hour, until firm enough to roll out, before using. (Or freeze for up to 2 months. Thaw in the refrigerator and let come to cool room temperature before using.)

Single crust, rye variation:
Reduce the all-purpose flour to 175 g (1¼ cups) and add 105 g (¾ cup) whole rye flour.

Single crust, lard variation:
Reduce the butter to 100 g (¼ cup + 3 Tbsp) and add 100 g (¼ cup + 3 Tbsp) of lard

---

Frangipane

Makes 460 g (2 cups)

This rich nut cream makes a beautiful filling for tarts and croissants. Customize it by changing the nut—ground toasted pecans, pistachios, hazelnuts, or even sunflower seeds. I have provided two methods: one uses a food processor, the other a hand mixer.

90 g (⅓ cup + 1 Tbsp) unsalted butter, softened

100 g (½ cup) sugar

½ tsp salt

2 large eggs

150 g (1¼ cups) ground almonds

2 Tbsp all-purpose flour

In a food processor fitted with the steel blade, combine all of the ingredients and process until well combined. Ta-da!

Or, in a large bowl, use a hand mixer to cream the butter with the sugar and salt, then add the eggs one by one. Fold in the ground almonds and flour until well combined.

Frangipane will keep for up to 5 days in an airtight container in the refrigerator.

Mixed Spice

Makes 60 mL (¼ cup)

I make a mixed spice concoction to use instead of measuring out multiple small amounts of spices in recipes like Hot Cross Buns (page 143) or Mincemeat (page 113). Use it where you would use pumpkin pie spice.

2 tsp whole cloves

6 allspice berries

1 star anise

3 green cardamom seeds (husk discarded)

3 blades of mace (optional)

1 Tbsp + 1 tsp cinnamon

1½ tsp ground ginger

1 tsp grated nutmeg

Use a spice grinder (mine doubles as my coffee grinder!) to finely grind the cloves, allspice, star anise, cardamom seeds, and mace, if using.

Transfer to a small jar and mix in the cinnamon, ginger, and nutmeg.

This will keep at room temperature in a tightly sealed jar for at least 6 months.

JAMES KEILLER & SON LTD. DUNDEE ORANGE MARMALADE · JAMES KEILLER DUNDEE · Keiller & Son Ltd · Lemon · SHELLING HALE'S GRATED PEACH · JAMES KEILLER DUNDEE ORANGE MARMALADE · FIVE

LA GROTTA · *Desserts* Nancy Silverton

The Violet Bakery Cookbook Claire Ptak · CHEZ PANISSE DESSERTS · LINDSEY REMOLIF SHERE PREFACE BY ALICE WATERS

Brooks Headley's **Fancy Desserts** · CHEZ PANISSE FRUIT · ALICE WATERS

THE LAST COURSE · CLAUDIA FLEMING WITH MELISSA CLARK · SLATER · *Ripe*

NANCY SILVERTON'S PASTRIES FROM THE LA BREA BAKERY · WEISS · CLASSIC GERMAN BAKING

❂ DUCHESS BAKE SHOP · Giselle Courteau · FRUIT · ALAN DAVIDSON

PAULA PECK · THE ART OF FINE BAKING

Preservation · preserving by the pint · The Art and Science of Cleaning, Preservation and Dehydration · FINE PRESERVING · The Jams and Jellies of Christine Ferber · PUTNAM · FISHER · Mes Confitures · SUE SHEPHARD · Pickled, Potted and Canned · How to Open a Financially Successful Bakery · Dianne Jacob · WILL *Write* FOR Food · ELIZABETH DAVID · An Omelette and a Glass of Wine · RUTH REICHL · Tender at the Bone · COMFORT ME WITH APPLES · RUTH REICHL · THE SOUL OF A CHEF · Jeffrey Steingarten · **Candyfreak** · It Must've Been Something I Ate · Steve Almond · THE DEVIL'S CUP · A JOURNEY THROUGH THE WORLD OF COFFEE · STEWART LEE ALLEN · IN THE DEVIL'S Garden · STEWART LEE ALLEN · Kitchen Confidential · Anthony Bourdain · MY LIFE IN FRANCE · JULIA CHILD with Alex Prud'homme · BLOOD, BONES & BUTTER · GABRIELLE HAMILTON · BRILLAT-SAVARIN · THE PHYSIOLOGY OF TASTE · ELIZABETH DAVID · ALLEN · MORE HOME COOKING · LAURIE COLWIN · THE RESOURCE GUIDE FOR FOOD WRITERS · COOKING AND DINING IN IMPERIAL ROME · PIE · Josef Chelsea · Visions of Sugarplums · Mimi Sheraton · Maida Heatter's Cakes · *Gourmet* THE GOURMET COOKIE BOOK · POTTER & SCOTT

T OF BAKING · ANNETTE WOLTER · CHRISTIAN TEUBNER · HPBooks · momofuku **milk bar** · christina tosi · Manzke

THE **CRAFT** OF BAKING · putting up · A Year-Round Guide to Canning · putting up more · SCANDINAVIAN BAKING · DAVID LEBOVITZ · TOAST & J · Sweet · MAGNOLIA · More from Magnolia · ROOM FO · RIPE · DOLCE ITALIA · ROBIC · COOKI · PATISSERIE MADE SIMPLE · AREFI · ZEGRL · BREAD, CAKE, DOUGHNUT · Ottolenghi & Goh · SWE · À LA MÈRE D · *The Secrets of Baking* · DESSERTS BY THE YARD · Patrice Demers · HOW TO BE · BAKING AND THE ART OF · baking at REPUB · CAKE BIBLE · ASIAN P

Resources

A brief list of my favorite books to enrich your preserving and baking journey.

Mes Confitures by Christine Ferber. I always dial back the sugar by at least 20% in her recipes, but she's a queen and this book is where I first really learned to make jam.

Saving the Season by Kevin West. A preserving book by a former *W* magazine editor?! This is a perfect blend of chic and down-home, filled with gorgeous photos and thoughtful essays.

Preserves by Pam Corbin (River Cottage Handbook No. 2). All of these recipes are beautiful and functional, especially if you fantasize about living in the English countryside (I know I do).

The Joy of Jams, Jellies, and Other Sweet Preserves by Linda Ziedrich. Ziedrich is such an amazing cookbook author, and here she plumbs the depths of sweet preserving.

Ripe by Nigel Slater. This book, by one of my favorite writers on food, bridges the gap—it's not about pastry or preserving (though it contains both), but is devoted to the love of FRUIT.

The Last Course by Claudia Fleming. A reissued classic that has finally been given its dues, this book has inspired me ever since I went on a pilgrimage to Gramercy Tavern to try her desserts.

Desserts and *Pastries from La Brea Bakery*, both by Nancy Silverton. Silverton is a pastry wizard, and these books are vital.

La Grotta Ices by Kitty Travers. This is a masterpiece on gelato and sorbet, well-written enough to read cover to cover like a novel.

Brooks Headley's Fancy Desserts by Brooks Headley. The writing is so excellent and so entertaining. He is unabashedly weird, and we need more of that.

Room for Dessert and *Ripe for Dessert* by David Lebovitz. These are two of the first pastry cookbooks I got, and I still go back to them.

I believe that one of the most dignified ways we are capable of, to assert and then reassert our dignity in the face of poverty and war's fears and pains, is to nourish ourselves with all possible skill, delicacy, and ever-increasing enjoyment.

—MFK FISHER

Acknowledgments

When I wrote my first cookbook, it felt like a dream come true, and I wanted nothing more than to immediately do it all over again, but better. Little did I know it would take many more years than I imagined for this wish to come to fruition. This was partly because of me and partly because of the changing publishing industry, and it might never have happened at all. I will be eternally grateful to everyone who helped this book see the light of day.

Thank You

To Allison Kave and Allison Day, two wonderful authors both named Allison who were so generous with advice about the mysterious world of book proposals and publishing.

To Jess Messer and family, for giving me the perfect quiet place to write in the most idyllic setting.

A million times thank you to Giselle Courteau, for all of the support and particularly, in this case, a vital referral.

To Robert McCullough for seeing *Jam Bake*'s potential, to my editor Katherine Stopa, and to all of the lovely team at Appetite by Random House.

To Michelle Marek, Stephanie Labelle, Natasha Pickowicz, and Laurel Wypkema for being amazing friends and pastry wizards, and for such generous recipe contributions. What an incredible gift!

To Susan Leclair, who was good enough to give me her pie recipe but to which I was not equal. And to Sandra Grant, for unearthing my favorite shortbread recipe.

To Maggie Boyd, bona fide artistic genius and incredible friend—having you illustrate this book is a dream come true.

To Mickael Bandassak. I am so lucky to have worked with such an amazing photographer. And to Michelle Marek again (!) for being a stylist beyond compare.

To Blake Mackay, my fellow teacher, for giving me a home away from home (thank you, Andrew, as well!) and lending lots of props and gear.

To Catherine Lepine Lafrance for so generously giving us a place to work.

To Merida Anderson, for the ceramics lent and the miniature miracle.

To Tave, Keegan, Tim, Kinneret, my downstairs neighbors, and many Toronto hospital staff for helping to consume so many of the pastries that threatened to overwhelm me during testing.

And last but never least, thank you to Kat Butler, my true love, for your enduring support and unwavering conviction that I am great.

Index